TEACHER'S PET PUBLICATIONS

LITPLAN TEACHER PACK

for

The Kite Runner

based on the book by

Khaled Hosseini

Written by

Christina Stone

TABLE OF CONTENTS
The Kite Runner

ABOUT THE AUTHOR

Khaled Hosseini

Khaled Hosseini was born in Kabul, Afghanistan, in 1965. His father was a diplomat with the Afghan Foreign Ministry, and his mother taught Farsi and History at a high school in Kabul. In 1976, Khaled moved to Paris with his family. They lived there for four years and instead of returning to a violent Afghanistan under Soviet control, sought political asylum in the United States in 1980.

Since the Hosseini family lost all their property in Afghanistan, they lived on welfare and food stamps for a short time when they first arrived in San Jose, California. Khaled's father worked several jobs to get his family off of welfare and provided Khaled with educational opportunities. Khaled graduated from high school in 1984 and earned his bachelor's degree in Biology from Santa Clara University in 1988. He continued his education at the University of California at San Diego, earning his Medical Degree in 1993.

Khaled was a practicing medical intern of internal medicine at the Cedars-Sinai Hospital in Los Angeles when he completed his first novel, *The Kite Runner*. This novel is semi-autobiographical; however, the story of Amir and Hassan is completely fictional.

Khaled has published a second novel, *A Thousand Splendid Suns,* and is know for being the first Afghan author to have his work published in English.

Major Works
The Kite Runner and *A Thousand Splendid Suns*

Awards
The Kite Runner has become an international bestseller, published in 38 countries. It has won the following awards and recognitions:
Book Sense Bestseller List Sensation
Boeke Prize
Barnes and Noble Discover Great New Writers Award
ALA Notable Book
Alex Award
Borders Original Voices Award 2003
Entertainment Weekly's Best Book 2003
San Francisco Chronicle Best Book of the Year 2003
Literature to Life Award

INTRODUCTION *The Kite Runner*

This LitPlan has been designed to develop students' reading, writing, thinking, and language skills through exercises and activities related to *The Kite Runner.* It includes twenty one lessons, supported by extra resource materials.

The **introductory lesson** provides students with background information about Afghanistan, the Soviet invasion, and the rise of the Taliban.

The **reading assignments** are approximately thirty pages each; some are a little shorter while others are a little longer. Students have approximately 15 minutes of pre-reading work to do prior to each reading assignment. This pre-reading work involves reviewing the study questions for the assignment and doing some vocabulary work for selected vocabulary words they will encounter in their reading.

The **study guide questions** are fact-based questions; students can find the answers to these questions right in the text. These questions come in two formats: short answer or multiple choice. The best use of these materials is probably to use the short answer version of the questions as study guides for students (since answers will be more complete), and to use the multiple choice version for occasional quizzes.

The **vocabulary work** is intended to enrich students' vocabularies as well as to aid in the students' understanding of the book. Prior to each reading assignment, students will complete a two-part worksheet for selected vocabulary words in the upcoming reading assignment. Part I focuses on students' use of general knowledge and contextual clues by giving the sentence in which the word appears in the text. Students are then to write down what they think the words mean based on the words' usage. Part II nails down the definitions of the words by giving students dictionary definitions of the words and having students match the words to the correct definitions based on the words' contextual usage. Students should then have an understanding of the words when they meet them in the text.

After each reading assignment, students will go back and formulate answers for the study guide questions. Discussion of these questions serves as a **review** of the most important events and ideas presented in the reading assignments.

After students complete reading the work, there is a **vocabulary review** lesson which pulls together all of the fragmented vocabulary lists for the reading assignments and gives students a review of all of the words they have studied.

Following the vocabulary review, a lesson is devoted to the **extra discussion questions/writing assignments**. These questions focus on interpretation, critical analysis and personal response, employing a variety of thinking skills and adding to the students' understanding of the novel.

There is a **cultural scrapbook project** in this unit. This project requires students to record information about the culture and traditions of Afghanistan in the novel and put together a scrapbook after doing additional research.

There are three **writing assignments** in this unit, each with the purpose of informing, persuading, or having students express personal opinions. The first writing assignment asks students write a creative short story, just as the protagonist does in the novel. The second writing assignment asks students to be Amir's conscience and convice him to help Hassan. In the third assignment students will write about a character in the novel explaining the most important things to know about this person.

There is a non-fiction **reading assignment**. Students must read non-fiction articles, books, etc. to gather information about their themes in our world today.

The **review lesson** pulls together all of the aspects of the unit. The teacher is given four or five choices of activities or games to use which all serve the same basic function of reviewing all of the information presented in the unit.

The **unit test** comes in two formats: multiple choice or short answer. As a convenience, two different tests for each format have been included. There is also an advanced short answer unit test for advanced students.

There are additional **support materials** included with this unit. The **Unit Resource Materials** section includes suggestions for an in-class library, crossword and word search puzzles related to the novel, and extra worksheets. There is a list of **bulletin board ideas** which gives the teacher suggestions for bulletin boards to go along with this unit. In addition, there is a list of **extra class activities** the teacher could choose from to enhance the unit or as a substitution for an exercise the teacher might feel is inappropriate for his/her class. **Answer keys** are located directly after the **reproducible student materials** throughout the unit. The **Vocabulary Resource Materials** section includes similar worksheets and games to reinforce the vocabulary words.

The **level** of this unit can be varied depending upon the criteria on which the individual assignments are graded, the teacher's expectations of his/her students in class discussions, and the formats chosen for the study guides, quizzes and test. If teachers have other ideas/activities they wish to use, they can usually easily be inserted prior to the review lesson.

UNIT OBJECTIVES *The Kite Runner*

1. Through reading the novel *The Kite Runner*, students will learn about the culture of Afghanistan and reexamine current Middle Eastern stereotypes Americans typically hold.
2. Students will demonstrate their understanding of the text on four levels: factual, interpretive, critical, and personal.
3. Students will make connections with the material in the text and apply the lessons learned to their lives.
4. Students will be given the opportunity to practice reading aloud and silently to improve their skills in each area.
5. Students will answer questions to demonstrate their knowledge and understanding of the main events and characters in *The Kite Runner* as they relate to the author's theme development.
6. Students will enrich their vocabularies and improve their understanding of the novel through the vocabulary lessons prepared for use in conjunction with the novel.
7. Students will demonstrate the ability to write effectively to inform by developing and organizing facts to convey information. Students will demonstrate the ability to write effectively to persuade by selecting and organizing relevant information, establishing an argumentative purpose, and by designing an appropriate strategy for an identified audience. Students will demonstrate the ability to write effectively to express personal ideas by selecting a form and its appropriate elements.
8. Students will read aloud, report, and participate in large and small group discussions to improve their public speaking and personal interaction skills.

READING ASSIGNMENTS *The Kite Runner*

Date Assigned	Assignment	Completion Date
	Assignment 1 Chapters 1-4	
	Assignment 2 Chapters 5-7	
	Assignment 3 Chapters 8-9	
	Assignment 4 Chapters 10-11	
	Assignment 5 Chapters 12-13	
	Assignment 6 Chapters 14-17	
	Assignment 7 Chapters 18-20	
	Assignment 8 Chapters 21-22	
	Assignment 9 Chapters 23-24	
	Assignment 10 Chapter 25	

UNIT OUTLINE *The Kite Runner*

1 Background DVD	2 Introduction PVR 1	3 Study ?s 1 Map PVR 2	4 Study ?s 2 Non-fication PVR 3	5 Writing Assignment #1
6 Study ?s 3 Birthdays PVR 4	7 Study ?s 4 Writing Assignment #2 PVR 5	8 Guest Speaker (s)	9 Study ?s 5 Weddings PVR 6	10 Study ?s 6 Rostam & Sohrab PVR 7
11 Study ?s 7 Afghan Stories PVR 8	12 Study ?s 8 PVR 9	13 Study ?s 9 Scrapbooks PVR 10	14 Study ?s 10 Character Studies	15 Writing Assignment #3
16 Vocabulary Review	17 Extra Discussion ?s	18 Extra Discussion ?s	19 Unit Review	20 Unit Tests
21 Afghanistan Day				

Key: P = Preview Study Questions V = Vocabulary Work R = Read

STUDY GUIDE QUESTIONS

STUDY GUIDE QUESTIONS *The Kite Runner*

Assignment 1
Chapters 1-4

1. What does Amir say happened to him at the age of twelve?
2. Compare and contrast the type of homes Amir and Hassan live in.
3. Who is Rahim Khan?
4. What happened to Amir's mother?
5. What happened to Hassan's mother?
6. Describe Ali.
7. What is physically odd about Hassan?
8. What did Amir's father build during Amir's early childhood?
9. Amir's father says there is only one sin in the world. What is it?
10. What favorite pastime does Amir have that his father just can't stand?
11. How did Amir's family come to know Ali?
12. What prompts Amir to write his first story?

Assignment 2
Chapters 5-7

1. What was the cause of all the gunfire and bombing that took place after Amir read Hassan his story?
2. What is Assef's reputation around town?
3. Assef says, "Too late for Hitler, but not for us." What does he mean?
4. What does Hassan do to save both himself and Amir from Assef?
5. What does Amir's father get Hassan for his birthday?
6. What is every kid's favorite season in Kabul?
7. What does it mean to "run" a kite?
8. Why do people have bloody hands after flying a kite?
9. What is the best prize to have during the kite fighting tournament?
10. Why does Amir want to win the kite tournament so badly?
11. What happens to Hassan after he has caught the last fallen kite from the tournament?
12. Why does Amir compare the look in Hassan's eyes while Assef is hurting him to the look in the lamb's eyes before it is killed for food?
13. What does Amir do when he sees what is happening to Hassan?

Assignment 3

<u>Chapters 8-9</u>

1. How does Hassan act in the weeks following the kite fighting tournament?
2. Describe Amir's relationship with his father after winning the tournament.
3. What did Amir say as he lay awake in the room of sleeping relatives in Jalalabad?
4. How does Hassan try to rekindle his relationship with Amir?
5. Amir and his father are enjoying their new relationship until Amir asks him a question that angers him. What is this question?
6. What occurs between Amir and Hassan at the top of the hill in the cemetery?
7. Describe Amir's birthday party.
8. Why does Amir get so angry when his father refers to Assef as Assef jan?
9. What gift does Assef give Amir for his birthday?
10. What story does Rahim tell Amir on his birthday?
11. What do Hassan and Ali give Amir for his birthday?
12. What does Amir do to get Ali and Hassan in trouble?
13. How does Amir's father react when Ali quits?

Assignment 4

<u>Chapters 10-11</u>

1. What is Karim's job?
2. To what country do Amir and his father first seek for safety from Afghanistan?
3. What country has a presence in Afghanistan as Amir and his father leave?
4. At the first checkpoint Amir's father stands up and confronts the Russian soldiers, putting himself in danger. Why?
5. Where do Amir and his father wait with the others trying to leave Afghanistan as new truck parts are ordered?
6. Amir listens to his father speak with Kamal's father. What does he say happened to Kamal?
7. How do Amir and his father travel on the second leg of their trip to safety?
8. When Amir's father tries to use a check to purchase food, he is shocked that he is asked for ID. He can't believe the lack of trust in America. Instead of a credit card, what method did they use in Afghanistan?
9. How does Amir's father react when he is given food stamps?
10. What does Amir do that prompts his father to tell him he is proud of his son?
11. Why does Amir's father buy an old Volkswagon bus?
12. What does Amir have a hard time forgetting about after leaving the flea market?

Assignment 5

Chapters 12-13

1. What harm can come from Amir talking to Soraya without the formal permission and supervision from her father?
2. What does Soraya's mother think of Amir's talking to her daughter without permission?
3. What does Soraya want to do with her life?
4. Compare and contrast how Amir and Soraya treated their illiterate servants when they were young.
5. What does General Taheri catch Amir giving to Soraya?
6. What does Amir find out about Baba's health?
7. What one last request does Amir have for his father after he is released from the hosptial?
8. What does Soraya confess to Amir?
9. Who does Amir wish was present at his wedding? Who does he wonder about at his wedding?
10. What does Soraya do while Amir is at work when they are first married?
11. What is Soraya's mother not allowed to ever do in public by orders of her husband?
12. What great accomplishment happens in regards to Amir's career?
13. What do Amir and Soraya try desperately to do, but are unsuccessful?

Assignment 6

Chapters 14-17

1. How does Amir find out Rahim Khan is sick?
2. What type of lifestyle do the Afghan people live in Pakistan?
3. How did Rahim get the scar on his face?
4. How did the people of Afghanistan react when the Taliban took control of the country?
5. How did Ali die?
6. What skill did Hassan learn later in life?
7. Where do Hassan and his family stay when they move back to Amir's home with Rahim?
8. Who shows up at Amir's old house one day in an old blue burqa?
9. How did Hassan's son get his name?
10. What does Rahim give Amir?
11. How did Hassan die?
12. What is Rahim's dying wish?
13. What shocking news does Rahim tell Amir?

Assignment 7

Chapters 18-20

1. What signs from his childhood does Amir think of that support the idea that his father is also Hassan's father?
2. Amir tells Rahim at first that he cannot go to Kabul because he has a wife in America, a home, a career, and a family. What makes him change his mind and go Kabul?
3. Who is Farid?
4. What does Amir have to wear as he travels to Kabul?
5. Describe the Afghanistan Amir sees upon his return.
6. Farid is resentful of Amir and treats him with contempt. What makes him suddenly change his attitude?
7. Amir thinks Wahid's children are envious of his wristwatch so he gives it to them as a gift. What does Amir later discover they really wanted?
8. How does Amir react the first time he sees the Taliban?
9. Whom does Amir meet who once knew his mother?
10. Why does the man at the orphanage say he has never seen Sohrab?
11. What does the director of the orphanage say happened to Sohrab?
12. Why does Farid try to kill the director of the orphanage?
13. How does Amir find Sohrab since Sohrab is gone form the orphanage?

Assignment 8

Chapters 21-22

1. What do Amir and Farid see two men haggling over in the street?
2. What does Amir look for when he climbs the hill to the cemetery where he and Hassan used to play?
3. Even though it is really hot, what are all the soccer players wearing?
4. What happens at half time during the soccer game?
5. Why doesn't Farid go with Amir to meet with the man in white with the sunglasses to ask about Sohrab?
6. Why could Amir be arrested for treason?
7. What does Sohrab to do when he enters the room when Amir sees him for the first time?
8. Who is the man with the sunglasses?
9. What does Amir have to do to "earn" Sohrab?
10. Why does Amir start laughing when he is in so much pain?
11. Describe how Amir is finally able to leave the room and get away to safety with Sohrab.

Assignment 9

Chapters 23-24

1. Describe some of Amir's most severe injuries.
2. What is the significance of Amir's injury to his lip?
3. What happened to Rahim Khan?
4. Why does Amir leave the hospital in Peshawar and go to Islamabad?

5. Amir planned on leaving Sohrab with the Caldwell family in Pakistan. Why does Amir suddenly have to change his plans and become responsible for Sohrab?
6. What does Amir give to Farid for helping him on his journey to find Sohrab?
7. Where does Sohrab go when he runs away from the hotel?
8. Why is Sohrab scared to go with Amir to America?
9. What does Amir discover at the American embassy when trying to get information about adopting Sohrab?
10. What does Sohrab do at the hotel each night before bed?
11. What suggestion does the immigration lawyer give to Amir as his best chance of getting Sohrab out of Afghanistan and into America?
12. What good news does Soraya give Amir?
13. What does Amir discover when he goes into the bathroom to talk to Sohrab?

Assignment 10

Chapter 25

1. What "bargain" does Amir make with God?
2. What did Sohrab do to himself?
3. What does Sohrab say he wants?
4. What does Sohrab's new room in America look like?
5. In what way does Amir stand up to the General for the first time?
6. Describe how Sohrab acts once in America.
7. What significant historical event happens a few months after Amir returns to America?
8. With what project does Amir get involved?
9. What celebration do Amir and his family attend?
10. What does Amir buy at this celebration?
11. What happens at this celebration that makes Sohrab smile?

STUDY GUIDE QUESTIONS ANSWER KEY *The Kite Runner*

Assignment 1
<u>Chapters 1-4</u>

1. What does Amir say happened to him at the age of twelve?
   Amir says that at the age of twelve he became the person he is today.
2. Compare and contrast the type of homes Amir and Hassan live in.
   Amir lives in one of the fanciest mansions in the city, while Hassan lives in a small mud hut on the same property.
3. Who is Rahim Khan?
   Rahim Khan is the best friend and business partner of Amir's father.
4. What happened to Amir's mother?
   She died of hemorrhaging giving birth to Amir.
5. What happened to Hassan's mother?
   She ran off with a clan of traveling singers and dancers five days after he was born.
6. Describe Ali.
   He is an honorable man who memorized the Koran. He is also partially crippled and the lower part of his face is crippled.
7. What is physically odd about Hassan?
   He has a cleft lip.
8. What did Amir's father build during Amir's early childhood?
   He built an orphanage, doing all of the design work on his own and funding it completely.
9. Amir's father says there is only one sin in the world. What is it?
   His father says that theft is the only sin. All other sins are just a variation of theft.
10. What favorite pastime does Amir have that his father just can't stand?
    Amir enjoys reading even though his father has tried very hard to make him like sports.
11. How did Amir's family come to know Ali?
    Ali's parents were hit by impaired drivers. The drivers were brought before Amir's grandfather, the judge, along with the orphaned son, Ali. After the trial, Amir's grandfather adopted Ali and he was raised alongside Amir's father.
12. What prompts Amir to write his first story?
    Amir pretends to be reading a book to Hassan but is really just making something up. Hassan loves the tale and says it's the best he's heard in a long time. This gives Amir confidence in his story-telling abilities and makes him sit down and write his own story.

Assignment 2
<u>Chapters 5-7</u>

1. What was the cause of all the gunfire and bombing that took place after Amir read Hassan his story?
   The monarchy had been overthrown in a coup.
2. What is Assef's reputation around town?
   He is a sociopath who carries brass knuckles with him and enjoys hurting others.
3. Assef says, "Too late for Hitler, but not for us." What does he mean?
   Assef wants the new leader of Afghanistan to get rid of all the Hazara descedents so that it is only the Pashtuns who are left.

4. What does Hassan do to save both himself and Amir from Assef?
He takes out his slingshot and aims a large rock at Assef's eye. Assef knows that if he moves to attack he will be blinded.
5. What does Amir's father get Hassan for his birthday?
Amir's father pays for Hassan to have surgery to fix his cleft lip.
6. What is every kid's favorite season in Kabul?
Winter is every kids favorite season, since school is out and that is the time of the kite tournament.
7. What does it mean to "run" a kite?
A kite runner is someone who runs all around the city trying to catch a falling kite before it lands.
8. Why do people have bloody hands after flying a kite?
The kite string is covered in glass to help cut down other kites and win the tournaments. When flying a kite and guiding it, the person's hands get cut from the glass on the string.
9. What is the best prize to have during the kite fighting tournament?
The most coveted prize is catching the last kite to fall from the sky.
10. Why does Amir want to win the kite tournament so badly?
Amir realizes this is a way to gain his father's love and affection and to finally make him proud.
11. What happens to Hassan after he has caught the last fallen kite from the tournament?
He is raped by Assef.
12. Why does Amir compare the look in Hassan's eyes while Assef is hurting him to the look in the lamb's eyes before it is killed for food?
Both have a look of acceptance and understanding of the situation and are resigned to enduring it for a higher purpose.
13. What does Amir do when he sees what is happening to Hassan?
Amir turns the other way and makes the choice to not help him.

Assignment 3

Chapters 8-9

1. How does Hassan act in the weeks following the kite fighting tournament?
Hassan does his chores and then sleeps as much as possible.
2. Describe Amir's relationship with his father after winning the tournament.
He and his father spend a lot of time together. They see movies together, visit the zoo, and go on trips. His father agrees to everything Amir asks, and the two talk more than ever.
3. What did Amir say as he lay awake in the room of sleeping relatives in Jalalabad?
Amir says he saw Hassan get raped, although no one hears it since they are all asleep.
4. How does Hassan try to rekindle his relationship with Amir?
Hassan seeks out Amir and asks him to run errands with him, but Amir refuses to go.
5. Amir and his father are enjoying their new relationship until Amir asks him a question that angers him. What is this question?
Amir asks his father if he's ever thought of getting new servants.
6. What occurs between Amir and Hassan at the top of the hill in the cemetery?
Amir and Hassan go to read, but Amir pummels Hassan with pomegranates over and over, asking him to fight back.

7. Describe Amir's birthday party.
   Amir's party is very extravagant. There are over 400 guests, the yard is decorated with lights, there is the finest food available, one of the most popular musicians in the country performs, and at the end there are fireworks.
8. Why does Amir get so angry when his father refers to Assef as Assef jan?
   The word "jan" is a term of endearment, one that Amir's father never uses when he talks to Amir.
9. What gift does Assef give Amir for his birthday?
   Assef gives him the biography of Hitler.
10. What story does Rahim tell Amir on his birthday?
    Rahim tells Amir he was once going to get married to a Hazara, but when his family found out they sent her away forever. He tells him it was probably for the best since she would have never been accepted.
11. What do Hassan and Ali give Amir for his birthday?
    Hassan and Ali give him a brand new copy of Shahnamah, *the favorite book of both boys. It has hand drawn illustrations and was most likely expensive.*
12. What does Amir do to get Ali and Hassan in trouble?
    Amir hides his new watch and some money under Hassan's mattress to make it look like he was stealing from them.
13. How does Amir's father react when Ali quits?
    He begs them not to leave and tells them they are forgiven. He cries, which is something Amir has never seen his father do.

Assignment 4

Chapters 10-11

1. What is Karim's job?
   He is a people smuggler. He gets people out of Afghanistan.
2. To what country do Amir and his father first seek for safety from Afghanistan?
   They head to Pakistan for safety.
3. What country has a presence in Afghanistan as Amir and his father leave?
   Russian soldiers are in Afghanistan during this time.
4. At the first checkpoint Amir's father stands up and confronts the Russian soldiers, putting himself in danger. Why?
   One of the Russian soldiers wants to rape an Afghan woman on the bus.
5. Where do Amir and his father wait with the others trying to leave Afghanistan as new truck parts are ordered?
   They wait crammed into a cold, dark basement with rats running around.
6. Amir listens to his father speak with Kamal's father. What does he say happened to Kamal?
   Kamal's father explains that Kamal was beaten up and raped by four people and no longer talks at all.
7. How do Amir and his father travel on the second leg of their trip to safety?
   They are put into an empty fuel tank with several others. There is absolutely no light, the air they breathe is full of gasoline fumes, and they cannot move or get out for quite some time.

8. When Amir's father tries to use a check to purchase food, he is shocked that he is asked for ID. He can't believe the lack of trust in America. Instead of a credit card, what method did they use in Afghanistan?
   They would snap a tree branch and use it as a credit card. The merchant would make a notch each time something was purchased and at the end of the month they would pay for the number of notches.
9. How does Amir's father react when he is given food stamps?
   Amir's father returns them and says that he will work for money for food and that he doesn't need charity.
10. What does Amir do that prompts his father to tell him he is proud of his son?
    When Amir graduates from high school his father tells him he is proud.
11. Why does Amir's father buy an old Volkswagon bus?
    He buys a bus so they can go to garage sales and load up on cheap stuff to sell for a profit at the flea market.
12. What does Amir have a hard time forgetting about after leaving the flea market?
    He can't forget a beautiful girl he met, Soraya Taheri.

Assignment 5

Chapters 12-13

1. What harm can come from Amir talking to Soraya without the formal permission and supervision from her father?
   Everyone would gossip about her and equate her to being "easy" for talking to him.
2. What does Soraya's mother think of Amir's talking to her daughter without permission?
   She adores Amir and has no problem with them talking to each other. She hopes he will fall for her daughter and be a suitor for her.
3. What does Soraya want to do with her life?
   She wants to be a teacher even though her mother and father would prefer her to be a doctor or lawyer.
4. Compare and contrast how Amir and Soraya treated their illiterate servants when they were young.
   Amir would make fun of Hassan for not knowing what words meant and would play games with him when reading so he would feel dumb. Soraya took great pleasure in teaching her servant to read and write so she could communicate with her sister.
5. What does General Taheri catch Amir giving to Soraya?
   The General catches Amir giving Soraya one of the short stories he wrote.
6. What does Amir find out about Baba's health?
   His father has Oat Cell Carcinoma, an advanced and inoperable form of cancer.
7. What one last request does Amir have for his father after he is released from the hosptial?
   Amir asks his father to arrange his marriage with Soraya.
8. What does Soraya confess to Amir?
   She tells him that she has been with another man. She explains that she ran away from home and lived with her boyfriend for a month until her father came and forced her to come home.
9. Who does Amir wish was present at his wedding? Who does he wonder about at his wedding?
   Amir wishes Rahim Khan was at his wedding and wonders if Hassan ever married.

10. What does Soraya do while Amir is at work when they are first married?
She takes care of Amir's father day and night. They live with him, and she does the cooking for him and administers his medicine. She also reads to him each day.
11. What is Soraya's mother not allowed to ever do in public by orders of her husband?
She is never allowed to sing in public, though she has a very beautiful voice.
12. What great accomplishment happens in regards to Amir's career?
He becomes a published author.
13. What do Amir and Soraya try desperately to do, but are unsuccessful?
They try very hard to have a child, but after expensive procedures and medications, nothing works.

Assignment 6

Chapters 14-17

1. How does Amir find out Rahim Khan is sick?
Rahim calls Amir and asks him to come to Pakistan to see him.
2. What type of lifestyle do the Afghan people live in Pakistan?
They are very poor. Some open businesses, but they are struggling to stay alive in very crowded areas.
3. How did Rahim get the scar on his face?
He was at a soccer game when the man next to him cheered loudly after a goal. Someone patrolling the game thought it was Rahim who made the noise and hit him in the face with his gun.
4. How did the people of Afghanistan react when the Taliban took control of the country?
They were happy, they celebrated and danced in the streets because they thought it was an end to the war and their country would once again know peace.
5. How did Ali die?
He was killed by a land mine.
6. What skill did Hassan learn later in life?
He learned to read and write.
7. Where do Hassan and his family stay when they move back to Amir's home with Rahim?
Hassan insists on living in the small hut and refuses to take a room in the house, even though Rahim pleads with him to do so.
8. Who shows up at Amir's old house one day in an old blue burqa?
Hassan's real mother shows up very sick and scarred from abuse. Hassan and his wife take her in and care for her. She eventually becomes part of the family and is very close with her grandson.
9. How did Hassan's son get his name?
He was named Sohrab after the boy in Amir and Hassan's favorite childhood story.
10. What does Rahim give Amir?
He gives him a photo of Hassan and his son along with a letter from Hassan to Amir.
11. How did Hassan die?
There was a rumor that a Hazara was living alone in the big house so the Taliban went to check it out. Hassan explained Rahim owned the house and was away to visit the doctor, but the Taliban did not believe him. They said they were moving in to the house and when Hassan protested they took him to the street and shot him in the head. His wife came out afterwards and was shot too.

12. What is Rahim's dying wish?
He wants Amir to go to Kabul and rescue Hassan's son from the orphanage. He wants Amir to bring him to Pakistan so he can live with an American couple who care for orphaned children.

13. What shocking news does Rahim tell Amir?
Rahim explains that Ali was sterile and could not have children. He then alludes to the fact that Amir's father was also Hassan's father. He had gotten Hassan's mother pregnant so Ali could have a child, and they kept it a secret all this time. Amir and Hassan were actually half brothers.

Assignment 7

<u>Chapters 18-20</u>

1. What signs from his childhood does Amir think of that support the idea that his father is also Hassan's father?
His dad paid for Hassan's harelip to be fixed, he never missed his birthday, he called Hassan "family" when Amir asked him if he would ever get new servants, and he cried the day Ali and Hassan left.

2. Amir tells Rahim at first that he cannot go to Kabul because he has a wife in America, a home, a career, and a family. What makes him change his mind and go Kabul?
Amir realizes that his actions years ago prevented Hassan from having those same things in his life. His father may have brought Hassan and Ali along with them to America, where Hassan could have the same things Amir had now. Knowing he may have prevented this, he feels he has to go.

3. Who is Farid?
Rahim introduced Amir to Farid, who was hired to drive Amir into Kabul. Farid lost his two youngest girls to a land mine blast and was injured by that same incident himself.

4. What does Amir have to wear as he travels to Kabul?
He must wear traditional Afghan clothing, though he never did when he actually lived in Afghanistan. He also has to wear a fake beard.

5. Describe the Afghanistan Amir sees upon his return.
Examples of poverty are everywhere. Homes have been destroyed by war and people are homeless, hungry, and without electricity. Taliban trucks patrol the streets looking for ways to exert their violence.

6. Farid is resentful of Amir and treats him with contempt. What makes him suddenly change his attitude?
Farid assumes Amir is going to sell his father's big house for money to take back to America to spend on lavish things like a vacation. When he finds out Amir is trying to rescue an orphan and get him to safety, he changes his attitude.

7. Amir thinks Wahid's children are envious of his wristwatch so he gives it to them as a gift. What does Amir later discover they really wanted?
He finds out the children were not looking at his watch but at the food he was eating. They were hungry for food, and Amir was unknowingly eating the last of it.

8. How does Amir react the first time he sees the Taliban?
He stares at the men passing by in the truck with guns. People around Amir scold him for looking directly at them, warning him that this may provoke them. Amir is filled with fear and can't quite get over seeing them in person rather than on the news.

9. Whom does Amir meet who once knew his mother?
Amir meets a homeless man on the street and finds out he was a professor with his mother.

10. Why does the man at the orphanage say he has never seen Sohrab?
He is afraid that Farid and Amir are here to bring him some harm, so he pretends to have never seen him.
11. What does the director of the orphanage say happened to Sohrab?
Once a month a Taliban official comes to the orphanage and takes a child for his pleasure. A month ago, this man took Sohrab.
12. Why does Farid try to kill the director of the orphanage?
He finds out that he is selling children for sexual purposes to the Taliban. This outrages him, and he jumps on the director and nearly kills him until Amir tells him the children are watching.
13. How does Amir find Sohrab since Sohrab is gone form the orphanage?
Amir is supposed to go to the soccer stadium the next day to look for the man with the dark sunglasses.

Assignment 8

Chapters 21-22

1. What do Amir and Farid see two men haggling over in the street?
Two men are haggling over an artificial leg. One man is selling his leg on the black market to get money for his family.
2. What does Amir look for when he climbs the hill to the cemetery where he and Hassan used to play?
He looks for the carving on the pomegranate tree that says, "Amir and Hassan, the Sultans of Kabul."
3. Even though it is really hot, what are all the soccer players wearing?
They are all wearing pants since the Taliban think shorts are too revealing.
4. What happens at half time during the soccer game?
The Taliban bring out a man and a woman and place them both in a chest-deep hole behind the goalpost. A leading member of the Taliban comes out and stones them to death as the crowd watches.
5. Why doesn't Farid go with Amir to meet with the man in white with the sunglasses to ask about Sohrab?
It is too dangerous for Farid. He thinks of himself and his family, and he is afraid.
6. Why could Amir be arrested for treason?
The Taliban think that those who leave the country to avoid fighting are committing treason. The man with the glasses asks Amir why he isn't fighting with his fellow Muslims, and tells him he could be arrested for treason for leaving to live in America.
7. What does Sohrab do when he enters the room when Amir sees him for the first time?
He is forced to dance to music. He is wearing a demeaning outfit and has bells strapped to his ankles.
8. Who is the man with the sunglasses?
He is Assef, the boy from Amir's childhood who raped Hassan.
9. What does Amir have to do to "earn" Sohrab?
He has to fight Assef. Assef reminds him they have unfinished business from when they were children, and in order to leave they must fight until one of them is killed.
10. Why does Amir start laughing when he is in so much pain?
He realizes that for the first time since the winter of 1975 he is at peace, even though he is getting severely beaten.

11. Describe how Amir is finally able to leave the room and get away to safety with Sohrab.
Sohrab picks up a brass ball off the bottom of the table and puts it in his slingshot. He asks Assef to stop, and when he doesn't he shoots him in the eye. Assef loses his eye and is in great pain.

Assignment 9

Chapters 23-24

1. Describe some of Amir's most severe injuries.
His mouth is wired shut from a broken jaw, he has a ruptured spleen, several broken ribs, a punctured lung, a broken bone around his eye socket, several missing teeth, and many cuts.
2. What is the significance of Amir's injury to his lip?
Hassan was harelipped and had a scar in the same place above his mouth. Now, Amir has the same exact scar that Hassan had.
3. What happened to Rahim Khan?
He left town the same day that Amir and Farid did. He left Amir a note and keys to a safety deposit box with money inside.
4. Why does Amir leave the hospital in Peshawar and go to Islamabad?
Farid thinks that Amir will not be safe in Peshawar. He knows the Taliban have friends and he is worried they will come looking for Amir. As soon as Amir is able to walk, they leave for a safer city.
5. Amir planned on leaving Sohrab with the Caldwell family in Pakistan. Why does Amir suddenly have to change his plans and become responsible for Sohrab?
The Caldwell family doesn't exist.
6. What does Amir give to Farid for helping him on his journey to find Sohrab?
He gives him all the money Rahim left, a little over $2,000.
7. Where does Sohrab go when he runs away from the hotel?
He goes to the large mosque, Shah Faisal.
8. Why is Sohrab scared to go with Amir to America?
He is afraid that Amir will get tired of him, or that Amir's wife won't like him.
9. What does Amir discover at the American embassy when trying to get information about adopting Sohrab?
Amir discovers that the process of getting Sohrab will be nearly impossible. The embassy suggests that he just give up. A lawyer Amir hires also suggests the same thing.
10. What does Sohrab do at the hotel each night before bed?
He takes a very long, hot bath.
11. What suggestion does the immigration lawyer give to Amir as his best chance of getting Sohrab out of Afghanistan and into America?
He says the best way to bring Sohrab home would be to relinquish him to an orphanage and start the paperwork through a private adoption agency after they do a home study.
12. What good news does Soraya give Amir?
She tells him her uncle who works for the INS is going to be able to get Sohrab into the country immediately and without any problems.
13. What does Amir discover when he goes into the bathroom to talk to Sohrab?
Sohrab is bleeding and unconscious in the tub.

Assignment 10

<u>Chapter 25</u>

1. What "bargain" does Amir make with God?
   He promises to think of Him every day and be a practicing Muslim if God will save Sohrab's life.
2. What did Sohrab do to himself?
   He used Amir's razor blade to try to commit suicide.
3. What does Sohrab say he wants?
   He tells Amir he is tired of everything and that he wants his old life back.
4. What does Sohrab's new room in America look like?
   Soraya decorated Sohrab's new room with sheets showing brightly colored kites. She also made a growing chart on the wall and had a wicker basket overflowing with toys.
5. In what way does Amir stand up to the General for the first time?
   The General calls Sohrab a Hazara boy, and Amir stands up to him telling him never to use that term in his presence again.
6. Describe how Sohrab acts once in America.
   Sohrab is silent. He never speaks to anyone and takes up very little space. He sleeps all the time and sometimes it is hard to remember he is even there.
7. What significant historical event happens a few months after Amir returns to America?
   The twin towers in New York City fall on September 11, 2001.
8. With what project does Amir get involved?
   He works to raise money and get grants for a hospital on the Afghanistan/Pakistan border.
9. What celebration do Amir and his family attend?
   Amir and his family go to the park to celebrate the Afghan New Year's Day on the first day of spring with others from Afghanistan.
10. What does Amir buy at this celebration?
    He buys a kite like the ones in Afghanistan so he can fight the other kites already flying in the sky.
11. What happens at this celebration that makes Sohrab smile?
    He flies a kite with Amir. The two fight another kite and win the tournament.

MULTIPLE CHOICE STUDY/QUIZ QUESTIONS
The Kite Runner

Assignment 1
Chapters 1-4

1. What does Amir say happened to him at the age of twelve?
   A. He saw something so devasting he will never forget it.
   B. He made a decision that will haunt him the rest of his life.
   C. He experienced the best day of his entire life.
   D. He became the person he is today.

2. Compare and contrast the type of homes Amir and Hassan live in.
   A. Amir lives in a gated community, while Hassan lives in a small apartment outside Kabul.
   B. Amir lives in a huge home, while Hassan lives in a compound for poor people.
   C. Amir lives in one of the fanciest mansions in the city, while Hassan lives in a small mud hut on the same property.
   D. Amir lives on a beautiful ranch, while Hassan lives in military housing.

3. Who is Rahim Khan?
   A. Amir's best friend growing up
   B. The best friend and business partner of Amir's father
   C. A political leader in Afghanistan
   D. Hassan's uncle who works for the government

4. What happened to Amir's mother?
   A. She dies of hemorrhaging while giving birth to Amir.
   B. She died from complications after a suicide bomber hit Amir's school.
   C. She ran away with another man when Amir was young.
   D. She was killed by the Taliban while at a peaceful protest.

5. What happened to Hassan's mother?
   A. She ran off with a clan of traveling singers and dancers.
   B. She was arrested on suspicion of treason.
   C. She died shortly after childbirth.
   D. She was murdered while walking home one night.

6. Describe Ali.

   A. He is an honorable man who memorized the Koran. He is also partially crippled and the lower part of his face is crippled.

   B. He is a highly educated man who has overcome many struggles in life. He is also one of the most handsome men in all of Kabul, and women dream about a life with him.

   C. He is a hard worker who has reached a successful position in his later life. He also is one of the few men in the city who comes from two different racial backgrounds.

   D. He is a lower class citizen who has committed crimes in the past but has worked to turn his life around. He also has a skin disease which creates an odd coloring of his skin.

7. What is physically odd about Hassan?

   A. His eyes are two different colors

   B. He has a cleft lip

   C. He is missing one leg

   D. One arm is noticeably smaller than the other

8. What did Amir's father build during Amir's early childhood?

   A. An orphanage

   B. A shopping center

   C. A hospital

   D. A school

9. Amir's father says there is only one sin in the world. What is it?

   A. Adultery

   B. Theft

   C. Greed

   D. Murder

10. What favorite pastime does Amir have that his father just can't stand?

   A. Magic

   B. Soccer

   C. Reading

   D. Golf

11. How did Amir's family come to know Ali?

A. Ali's parents were arrested for aiding the government. Amir's grandfather handled the court case and sentenced them to death. He felt sorry for their son, who was not involved, and adopted Ali, who was raised alongside Amir's father.

B. Ali's parents were very wealthy and traveled for business quite often. They constantly left Hassan home alone and one day decided to send him to live with his good friend from school, Amir's father. He ended up living with them and the two were raised together.

C. Ali's parents were hit by impaired drivers. The drivers were brought before Amir's grandfather, the judge, along with the orphaned son, Ali. After the trial, Amir's grandfather adopted Ali, and he was raised alongside Amir's father.

D. Ali's parents were very poor and could not afford to feed and house their son. Each day, they watched as Amir's grandfather walked out of the courthouse and to his expensive car. One day they stopped him and begged him to take Hassan, who was then raised alongside Amir's father.

12. What prompts Amir to write his first story?

A. Amir has a very vivid dream that he can't get out of his mind for weeks. He tells both his father and Hassan about the dream, and they encourage him to pick up a pen and record the dream. As he is doing this, he turns it into a story.

B. Amir overhears his father talking business with some very important people in Afghanistan. Amir can't help but think how this meeting resembled children fighting in the schoolyard and decides to write a story bringing the two scenarios together.

C. Amir pretends to be reading a book to Hassan but is really just making something up. Hassan loves the tale and says it's the best he's heard in a long time. This gives Amir confidence in his story-telling abilities and encourages him to write his own story.

D. Amir's teacher requires everyone in the class to write a short paragraph and read it to the class. The class cheers loudly after Amir reads his paragraph and tells him to continue the story. This makes Amir feel proud and prompts him to write a full short story.

Assignment 2
Chapters 5-7

1. What was the cause of all the gunfire and bombing that took place after Amir read Hassan his story?
   A. The Taliban tried to take control of the government but failed.
   B. The monarchy had been overthrown in a coup.
   C. The people were celebrating in the streets over finding more oil near the base of the mountain range.
   D. The Pakistani people were invading the streets of Kabul in a fight for land and resources.

2. What is Assef's reputation around town?
   A. He is the son of a wealthy businessman who wears American clothes and has American toys. He is thought to be the richest boy in Kabul.
   B. He is a quiet, thin boy who is known for being picked on by bullies.
   C. He is the smartest boy in town and is rumored to have been offered a scholarship to an American university.
   D. He is a sociopath who carries brass knuckles with him and enjoys hurting others.

3. Assef says, "Too late for Hitler, but not for us." What does he mean?
   A. Assef thinks the people of Afghanistan need to overthrow the current government to get rid of a leader who resembles Hitler in his manner of governing.
   B. Assef wants the new leader of Afghanistan to get rid of all the Hazara descedents so that it is only the Pashtuns who are left.
   C. Assef wants the new leader of Afghanistan to follow Hitler's lead and revolutionize their country. He thinks Hitler was able to lead his people in a way that the Afghan leader should.
   D. Assef thinks the people of Afghanistan need to find a leader who acts like Hitler in order to rid their country of foreigners who are trying to take control.

4. What does Hassan do to save both himself and Amir from Assef?
   A. He takes out his slingshot and aims a rock at Assef's eye. Assef knows that if he moves to attack he will be blinded.
   B. He pulls a gun out of his waistband and threatens to shoot Assef. Even though the gun isn't loaded, the trick works.
   C. He sacrifices the honor of his family and admits to Assef that his mother was a tramp who disgraced her whole family.
   D. He uses his powerful speaking ability to persuade Assef to let them go in exchange for the kite they were carrying which was worth nearly $75.

5. What does Amir's father get Hassan for his birthday?
   A. He buys him a very expensive kite that all the other boys covet.
   B. He pays for Hassan to have surgery to fix his cleft lip.
   C. He takes Hassan to a soccer game and helps him meet his favorite player.
   D. He opens a savings account for Hassan's future college expenses.

6. What is every kid's favorite season in Kabul?
   A. Summer
   B. Fall
   C. Spring
   D. Winter

7. What does it mean to "run" a kite?
   A. A kite runner is someone who has won at least three fighting tournaments.
   B. A kite runner is someone who helps the flyer get the kite in the air by running until the wind catches it.
   C. A kite runner is someone who runs all around the city trying to catch a falling kite before it lands.
   D. A kite runner is someone who sells fighting kites to people to enter in the tournament.

8. Why do people have bloody hands after flying a kite?
   A. The kite string is covered in glass to help cut down other kites and win the tournaments. When flying a kite and guiding it, the person's hands get cut from the glass on the string.
   B. In order to enter a kite fighting tournament one must make a blood pact to play by the rules. Anyone entering makes a small cut on their palm and then shakes hands with the others in the tournament.
   C. The kite flyer must use a very sharp knife to cut the string of his kite when it is caught with other objects. Since they are working fast to get the kite repaired and back in the air, kite flyers usually have bloody hands.
   D. The kite string is made of a fine silk that cuts into the kite flyer's hands causing them to bleed.

9. What is the best prize to have during the kite fighting tournament?
   A. The most coveted prize is catching the first kite to fall from the sky.
   B. The most coveted prize is to have the winning kite in the tournament.
   C. The most coveted prize is catching the last kite to fall from the sky.
   D. The most coveted prize is to collect the final two kites in the competition.

10. Why does Amir want to win the kite tournament so badly?
    A. Amir realizes this is a way to gain his father's love and affection and finally make him proud.
    B. Amir thinks this will help him win the attention of girls.
    C. Amir really wants to win the $1000 prize so he can buy more books.
    D. Amir believes this is the best way for him and Hassan to become better friends.

11. What happens to Hassan after he has caught the last fallen tournament kite?
    A. He is stabbed in a fight for possession of the kite.
    B. He is granted a kiss from a mysterious girl.
    C. He is awarded $50 from Amir for getting him the kite.
    D. He is raped by Assef.

12. Why does Amir compare the look in Hassan's eyes while Assef is hurting him to the look in the lamb's eyes before it is killed for food?
    A. Both have a look of acceptance and understanding and are resigned to enduring it for a higher purpose.
    B. Both have a look of being completely unaware of what is about to happen.
    C. Both have a look that is accusing others of guilt, making them feel remorse for what they are about to do.
    D. Both have a look of extreme sadness and pain that is hard for anyone watching to forget.

13. What does Amir do when he sees what is happening to Hassan?
    A. He yells at Assef to stop but Assef won't listen.
    B. He runs to go get help but is too late.
    C. He charges Assef and knocks him over, hoping Hassan will run away.
    D. He turns the other way and makes the choice to not help Hassan.

Assignment 3
Chapters 8-9

1. How does Hassan act in the weeks following the kite fighting tournament?
   A. Hassan begs Amir to go with him to the police.
   B. Hassan acts no differently than before.
   C. Hassan does his chores and then sleeps as much as possible.
   D. Hassan cries each night and visits the doctor several times.

2. Describe Amir's relationship with his father after winning the kite tournament.
   A. He and his father spend a lot of money. His father takes Amir with him to buy a new sports car, Amir gets new "American" clothes, and they buy a color TV for Amir's bedroom.
   B. He and his father are still not that close. Though Amir's father brags about Amir's win to others, he still doesn't talk to Amir at dinner, and he often goes to his study to be alone.
   C. He and his father do everything together. His father takes Amir with him to work to show off his son who won the tournament, also, Amir's father invites Amir to sit with him and Rahim in the study as they smoke cigars in the evening.
   D. He and his father spend a lot of time together. His father takes Amir to the movies, they visit the zoo, and go on trips.

3. What did Amir say as he lay awake in the room of sleeping relatives in Jalalabad?
   A. He saw Hassan get raped.
   B. He wishes he father loved him.
   C. He hates having Hassan and Ali as servants.
   D. He wishes he were dead.

4. How does Hassan try to rekindle his relationship with Amir?
   A. Hassan asks Amir's father to talk to Amir, but Amir makes excuses about being too busy for Hassan.
   B. Hassan asks Amir to run errands with him, but Amir refuses to go.
   C. Hassan buys Amir candy when he is in town, but Amir refuses to take it.
   D. Hassan has Ali go to Amir and explain that their friendship means a lot, but Amir ignores him.

5. Amir and his father are enjoying their new relationship until Amir asks him a question that angers him. What is this question?
   A. If he's ever thought about moving to America
   B. If he's ever thought about adopting Hassan
   C. If he's ever thought of getting new servants
   D. If he's ever thought about getting remarried

6. What occurs between Amir and Hassan at the top of the hill in the cemetery?
   A. Amir pummels Hassan with pomegranates over and over, taunting him to fight back.
   B. Amir cries when Hassan mentions the kite tournament, then runs away in shame before Hassan can figure out why.
   C. Amir punches Hassan and rubs his face in the dirt.
   D. Amir tells Hassan he saw him get raped, and dares him to tell on him for not helping him get away.

7. Describe Amir's birthday party.
   A. Amir's party is very American. A band performs popular American music, the yard is decorated with red, white, and blue streamers, they cook hamburgers and hotdogs, and sing happy birthday to Amir as he blows out the candles on his cake.
   B. Amir's party is very extravagant. There are over 400 guests, the yard is decorated with lights, the finest food available, one of the most popular musicians in the country performs, and at the end there are fireworks.
   C. Amir's party is very grown-up. Everyone shows up in tuxedos and ball gowns, an orchestra entertains everyone, the food served is a popular Afghan delicacy, and at the end everyone congratulates Amir in a champagne toast.
   D. Amir's party is very childish. There are nearly 200 children. 7 clowns entertain everyone, a popular magician performs, and at the end his father surprises Amir and his guests with pony rides.

8. Why does Amir get so angry when his father refers to Assef as Assef jan?
   A. The word "jan" is a term of anger, one that Amir knows will insult Assef and make him even more violent towards Hassan.
   B. The word "jan" is directed at young children and Amir feels his father is patronizing Assef when he uses this word.
   C. The word "jan" is a racial remark, and Amir is embarrassed his father is so openly making fun of Assef's light skin and blond hair.
   D. The word "jan" is a term of endearment, one that Amir's father never uses when he talks to Amir.

9. What gift does Assef give Amir for his birthday?
   A. Brass knuckles
   B. Hassan's bloody shirt
   C. The biography of Hitler
   D. American jeans

10. What story does Rahim tell Amir on his birthday?

   A. He was once a bully like Assef, but as he grew older he learned to control his temper.

   B. He was once going to get married to a Hazara, but when his family found out they sent her away forever.

   C. His brother was raped like Hassan and never could get over what happened to him.

   D. His mother was a Hazara, but he was too ashamed to tell anyone he knew since it would hurt his status in society.

11. What do Hassan and Ali give Amir for his birthday?

   A. A brand new copy of *Shahnamah* with hand drawn illustrations that was most likely expensive

   B. An old bike that Ali and Hassan repainted and fixed up

   C. A basket of fresh naan that Ali and Hassan prepared

   D. An obviously cheap but new journal

12. What does Amir do to get Ali and Hassan in trouble?

   A. Amir writes letters from a fake mistress addressed to Ali to make it look like Ali is unworthy of working in such a respected household.

   B. Amir hides his new watch and some money under Hassan's mattress to make it look like he was stealing from them.

   C. Amir records Hassan making rude comments about Assef and tells his father he was disrespecting an honored family friend.

   D. Amir goes around the house making a mess to make it look like Ali isn't able to do his job.

13. How does Amir's father react when Ali quits?

   A. He laughs and tells him he was already fired

   B. He refuses to pay them for the last month

   C. He begs them not to leave and cries

   D. He hurries them out of the house so no one will know

Assignment 4
Chapters 10-11

1. What is Karim's job?
   A. He is a people smuggler. He gets people out of Afghanistan.
   B. He is the chief of police. He works to make sure the Afghan people aren't mistreated while detained in prison.
   C. He is a crooked checkpoint officer. He allows people to leave Afghanistan if they pay him a substantial fee.
   D. He is the leader of an underground militia. He coordinates attacks against the government.

2. To what country do Amir and his father first seek for safety from Afghanistan?
   A. Pakistan
   B. Israel
   C. Iran
   D. Iraq

3. What country has a presence in Afghanistan as Amir and his father leave?
   A. Germany
   B. America
   C. Russia
   D. France

4. What problem occurs at the first checkpoint?
   A. One woman on the bus goes into labor as they approach the checkpoint. The driver wants to leave the woman and her husband on the side of the road to avoid any problems, but Amir's father refuses to let that happen.
   B. One of the soldiers wants to rape an Afghan woman on the bus, but Amir's father stands up and refuses to let it happen.
   C. Three people on the bus don't have the proper paperwork to leave the country. The soldiers threaten to shoot them for trying to leave illegally, but Amir's father is able to bribe them, and then allow the bus to get through.
   D. The soldiers require a bribe to get through the checkpoint. There was confusion about how much had to be paid and Amir's father has to give them an additional fee.

5. Where do Amir and his father wait with the others trying to leave Afghanistan as new truck parts are ordered?
   A. The attic of an abandoned house
   B. A rat infested basement
   C. A small cave near the border
   D. An underground tunnel

6. Amir listens to his father speak with Kamal's father. What does he say happened to Kamal?

   A. He was beaten up and raped by four people.
   B. He talked back to a soldier and they cut out his tongue.
   C. He was forced to watch as his wife and children were shot in the street.
   D. He stepped on a land mine and lost his leg.

7. How do Amir and his father travel on the second leg of their trip to safety?

   A. They are put into an empty fuel tank with several others. There is absolutely no light, the air they breathe is full of gasoline fumes, and they cannot move or get out for quite some time.
   B. They must crawl through an intricate tunnel system. There is no light, and they must crawl for days, unable to stand or stretch, with no food and minimal water.
   C. They must hike through steep, mountainous areas where there are no checkpoints since travel in this area is so dangerous. They deal with sand storms and harsh winds, nearly dying from the weather conditions.
   D. They lie on a pile of bodies being taken to burial. They have to remain still and endure the awful stench of rotting bodies as they travel across the border.

8. When Amir's father tries to use a check to purchase food, he is shocked that he is asked for ID. He can't believe the lack of trust in America. Instead of a credit card, what method did they use in Afghanistan?

   A. They would bring items to exchange instead of money. They would offer the merchant something he needed and in return would be given the item they needed.
   B. They would give the merchant money at the beginning of each month. As they visited they gave their name and money was deducted from their account until it came time to add more money to the account.
   C. They would snap a tree branch and use it as a credit card. The merchant would make a notch each time something was purchased, and at the end of the month they would pay for the number of notches.
   D. They would give the merchant a valuable item in exchange for the goods they needed. At the end of the month they would pay him the sum owed and could get their valuable items back.

9. How does Amir's father react when he is given food stamps?

   A. He is confused about how they work and doesn't understand how to use them. Several stamps go to waste from not being used in time.
   B. He returns them and says that he will work for money for food. He says he doesn't need charity.
   C. He agrees to use them but promises that he will donate the same dollar amount he uses in food stamps once he is financially sound in America.
   D. He is thankful that America has a system in place to help newcomers get on their feet.

10. What does Amir do that prompts his father to tell him he is proud of his son?
    A. Wins an award for a short story he wrote
    B. Graduates from high school
    C. Gets accepted into a good college
    D. Finds a respectable girl to marry

11. Why does Amir's father buy an old Volkswagon bus?
    A. So they can take a trip together and see more of America
    B. So they can move all of Amir's furniture and clothes into his college dorm
    C. So they can go to garage sales and load up on cheap stuff to sell for a profit at the flea market
    D. So they can drive more people in an Afghanistan carpool to the Mosque each week

12. What does Amir have a hard time forgetting about after leaving the flea market?
    A. A kite that looked exactly like the one he had in Afghanistan
    B. A man who made a racial comment to his father
    C. A collection of books that reminded him of those left behind in Afghanistan in his mother's library
    D. A beautiful girl he met

Assignment 5
Chapters 12-13

1. What harm can come from Amir talking to Soraya without the formal permission and supervision from her father?
   A. Everyone would gossip about her and equate her to being "easy" for talking to him.
   B. He can be accused of having improper intentions and can be harassed by others for trying to take advantage of an innocent girl.
   C. Soraya's father can become offended about their sneaking around and refuse to trust Amir with his daughter.
   D. Everyone would consider Amir dishonorable for not having permission from both families to begin courting a girl.

2. What does Soraya's mother think of Amir's talking to her daughter without permission?
   A. She has no problem with it and hopes the two will get married.
   B. She is offended that Amir would be so bold, and she doesn't approve of the relationship.
   C. She has mixed feelings about Amir and thinks their conversation is acceptable as long as she supervises.
   D. She is worried they will move too fast but does not forbid it since her daughter seems happy.

3. What does Soraya want to do with her life?
   A. Be a teacher
   B. Be a lawyer
   C. Be a doctor
   D. Be a vetrinarian

4. Compare and contrast how Amir and Soraya treated their illiterate servants when they were young.
   A. Amir and Soraya both believed their servants were not worthy of an education and treated them with little respect.
   B. Amir and Soraya both secretly read to their servants and helped educate them even though it was not an accepted practice.
   C. Amir made fun of Hassan for not knowing what words meant and made him feel dumb while Soraya taught her servant to read and write.
   D. Amir would help Hassan learn to read and write after school while Soraya didn't believe servants should be educated.

5. What does General Taheri catch Amir giving to Soraya?
   A. A short story he wrote
   B. A book of love poems
   C. A gold necklace with her birthstone
   D. A bus map with money to meet him later that night

6. What does Amir find out about Baba's health?
   A. Baba's mind is going and soon he will have a hard time taking care of himself.
   B. Baba has an advanced form of cancer that cannot be cured.
   C. Baba has heart problems and will most likely need a transplant.
   D. Baba has hip problems that will prevent him from heavy exercise in the future.

7. What one last request does Amir have for his father after he is released from the hospital?
   A. To give up smoking so he may live longer
   B. To contact Hassan to see if he is okay
   C. To read one of his short stories
   D. To arrange a marriage with Soraya

8. What does Soraya confess to Amir?
   A. That she is unable to have children
   B. That she has been with another man
   C. That she is not a practicing Muslim
   D. That she has a young child from a previous relationship

9. Who does Amir wish was present at his wedding? Who does he wonder about at his wedding?
   A. Amir wishes Hassan was at his wedding and wonders what ever happened to Assef.
   B. Amir wishes his entire family from Afghanistan was at his wedding and wonders if Hassan ever married.
   C. Amir wishes Rahim Khan was at his wedding and wonders if Hassan ever married.
   D. Amir wishes his mother was at his wedding and wonders if Rahim Khan is still alive.

10. What does Soraya do while Amir is at work when they are first married?
   A. She volunteers with a group to help other Afghan people get settled in America.
   B. She takes care of Amir's father day and night.
   C. She works at a daycare to earn extra money.
   D. She goes to college to work on her degree.

11. What is Soraya's mother never allowed to do in public by orders of her husband?
   A. Begin a conversation
   B. Read
   C. Smile
   D. Sing

12. What great accomplishment happens in regards to Amir's career?
   A. He makes over $100,000 a year.
   B. He is made partner at a law firm.
   C. He wins the Pulitzer Prize.
   D. He becomes a published author.

13. What do Amir and Soraya try desperately to do, but are unsuccessful?
   A. Adopt a child
   B. Have a child
   C. Move to New York
   D. Visit Afghanistan to see family

Assignment 6
Chapters 14-17

1. How does Amir find out Rahim Khan is sick?
   A. Rahim's doctor calls from Pakistan urging Amir to come quickly.
   B. Rahim writes a letter to Amir asking him to come to Pakistan before he dies.
   C. Rahim calls Amir and asks him to come to Pakistan to see him.
   D. Hassan sends Amir a letter informing him of Rahim's condition.

2. What type of lifestyle do the Afghan people live in Pakistan?
   A. They are very wealthy. Their money and valuables from Afghanistan are worth more in Pakistan, which is why so many relocate to this area.
   B. They are very poor. Some open businesses, but they are struggling to stay alive in very crowded areas.
   C. They are viewed as criminals. Many of them steal to survive and several have formed gangs with other Afghan people to take advantage of the Pakistani people.
   D. They are mostly middle class workers who run food marts and hotels in order to provide a comfortable living for their families.

3. How did Rahim get the scar on his face?
   A. He was at a soccer game when a man with the Taliban hit him in the face with his gun.
   B. He was robbed while walking home from the doctor and was cut with the knife of one of the men.
   C. He was at the market when a bomb went off and was hit with a piece of shrapnel.
   D. He had a cancerous tumor removed from the side of his face.

4. How did the people of Afghanistan react when the Taliban took control of the country?
   A. They were so happy they celebrated and danced in the streets.
   B. They were so upset many rioted and protested in the streets.
   C. They were worried about the state of the country and many fled for safety elsewhere.
   D. They were overjoyed and offered gifts of joy to the Taliban as they moved in to the city.

5. How did Ali die?
   A. He had a heart attack in his old age.
   B. He was killed by a land mine.
   C. He was shot by the Russians.
   D. He killed himself after hearing about the death of Amir's father.

6. What skill did Hassan learn later in life?
   A. He learned to paint.
   B. He learned to successfully harvest fruits and vegtables.
   C. He learned how to breed livestock.
   D. He learned to read and write.

7. Where do Hassan and his family stay when they move back to Amir's home with Rahim?
   A. In the basement of the house
   B. In the small hut Hassan was raised in
   C. In the guest house out back
   D. In the upstairs portion of the house

8. Who shows up at Amir's old house one day in an old blue burqa?
   A. Amir's mother
   B. Hassan's mother
   C. A mistress of Amir's father
   D. The woman Rahim nearly married years ago

9. How did Hassan's son get his name?
   A. After Hassan's great grandfather
   B. After Hassan's favorite character in a children's story
   C. After Amir's father
   D. After Hassan's favorite character in an old Western movie

10. What does Rahim give Amir?
    A. A letter from Hassan to Amir and the old kite Amir won in their last tournament
    B. An old banknote proving Amir's ownership to the house he grew up in and $2000
    C. A photo of Hassan and his son and the slingshot Hassan used to carry with him as a child
    D. A photo of Hassan and his son and a letter from Hassan to Amir

11. How did Hassan die?
    A. He was killed by a suicide bomber in the market.
    B. He was shot in the street by the Taliban.
    C. He died from an infection after his leg was amputated.
    D. He was arrested by the Taliban and later died from starvation while in prison.

12. What is Rahim's dying wish?

   A. For Amir to bring his wife to Pakistan to meet Rahim
   B. For Amir to rescue Hassan's son from the orphanage in Kabul and bring him to Pakistan
   C. For Amir to sell the house he owns and use the money to fund a children's hospital in Kabul
   D. For Amir to bring his father's body to Afghanistan to bury his body in the country he loved

13. What shocking news does Rahim tell Amir?

   A. That Amir's mother is also Hassan's mother; they are half brothers
   B. That Amir's parents could not have children; Amir is adopted
   C. That Amir's mother gave birth to twins, but one was sent away since they could not afford to care for two children
   D. That Amir's father is also Hassan's father; they are half brothers

Assignment 7
Chapters 18-20

1. What signs from his childhood does Amir think of that support this idea that his father is also Hassan's father?
   A. His dad used the term "jan" when he talked to Hassan, he took Hassan on private trips every month, he always threw Hassan an elaborate birthday party, and he paid to have Hassan privately educated.
   B. His dad showered Hassan with gifts, he invited Hassan into his study while he smoked cigars, he wrote letters to Hassan after they moved to America, and he asked Rahim to open the house to Hassan and his family.
   C. His dad paid for Hassan's harelip to be fixed, he never missed his birthday, he called Hassan family when Amir asked him if he would ever get new servants, and he cried the day Ali and Hassan left.
   D. He always played with Hassan more, he bragged about Hassan's accomplishments to others, he bought him gifts, and he sent him money each month after they moved to America.

2. Amir tells Rahim at first that he cannot go to Kabul because he has a wife in America, a home, a career, and a family. What makes him change his mind and go Kabul?
   A. Amir realizes that his actions years ago prevented Hassan from having those same things in his life.
   B. Amir believes that he would be dishonoring his father if he does not do this.
   C. Amir understands that Soraya would be ashamed of him if he did not do this, and he doesn't want to jeopardize their happy marriage.
   D. Amir knows this is the only way he can make up for his sins and not be condemned in the afterlife.

3. Who is Farid?
   A. The man driving Amir to Kabul
   B. The man who runs the orphanage where Sohrab was rumored to be
   C. The officer who allows Amir into Afghanistan even though he doesn't have permission from the government
   D. The leader of the Taliban

4. What does Amir have to wear as he travels to Kabul?
   A. He must wear a long robe and a backpack
   B. He must wear long pants and a head piece
   C. He must wear traditional Afghan clothing and a fake beard
   D. He must wear a burqa to cover his face and sandals

5. Describe the Afghanistan Amir sees upon his return.

   A. Poverty is everywhere. Most of the city is destroyed, and the Taliban roam the streets looking for trouble.

   B. The country is a mix of mansions and shacks. The Pashtun people are thriving and doing well in their businesses, while the Hazara people are living in poverty.

   C. The country is rebuilding. Many people have reopened shops and businesses and are returning to their homes.

   D. Wealth is everywhere. The country has discovered oil and is making a large profit by exporting it to other countries. Even the lower class people are doing well with all the jobs the oil rigs have brought to the area.

6. Farid is resentful of Amir and treats him with contempt. What makes him suddenly change his attitude?

   A. When he finds out Amir is a famous author back in the United States

   B. When he finds out his father and Amir's father used to be good friends

   C. When he finds out Amir is wealthy and will be paying him a large sum

   D. When he finds out Amir is trying to rescue an orphan and get him to safety

7. Amir thinks Wahid's children are envious of his wristwatch so he gives it to them as a gift. What does Amir later discover they really want?

   A. His food

   B. His clean clothes

   C. His ring

   D. His shoes

8. How does Amir react the first time he sees the Taliban?

   A. He hides his face immediately to avoid confrontation. He is nervous his face will give him away, letting the Taliban know he is not supposed to be there.

   B. He stares at the men as they drive by. He is filled with fear and can't quite get over seeing them in person rather than on the news.

   C. He yells angrily at them along with others who are standing on the street corner. They are not afraid since there are more citizens than Taliban.

   D. He runs into an alleyway to avoid their random violence. He is terrified that a stray bullet will hit him as he is running for safety.

9. Whom does Amir meet who once knew his mother?

   A. A homeless man who used to be a professor

   B. A hotel owner who once lived next door

   C. A Taliban officer

   D. A retired doctor who treated his mother

10. Why does the man at the orphanage say he has never seen Sohrab?
   A. He is afraid that they are going to hurt him.
   B. He is holding out for a bribe since he is desperate for money.
   C. He is having a bad day and takes it out on Amir.
   D. He is worried they will take Sohrab who is his favorite child.

11. What does the director of the orphanage say happened to Sohrab?
   A. A man from the Taliban occasionally comes to take a child for his personal pleasure. Sohrab was the child he chose to take the last time.
   B. Sohrab had special needs and was sent to an orphanage that could provide him with the medical care he needed.
   C. The Taliban came in shooting Hazara children. Sohrab was able to escape and has not been heard of since.
   D. The kids all made fun of Sohrab and beat him up repeatedly. Sohrab fought back injuring four kids with his slingshot and ran away.

12. Why does Farid try to kill the director of the orphanage?
   A. He is outraged that many children are starving and have no real beds to sleep in.
   B. He finds out he is allowing children to abuse each other physically.
   C. He is outraged that the man will not help them find Sohrab.
   D. He finds out that he is selling children for sexual purposes to the Taliban.

13. How does Amir find Sohrab since Sohrab is gone from the orphanage?
   A. He gets $3000 and comes back the next day.
   B. He travels to another orphanage to check to see if Sohrab is there.
   C. He meets a man with dark sunglasses at the soccer stadium the next day.
   D. He finds a man in a red robe at a kabob house later that night.

Assignment 8
Chapters 21-22

1. What do Amir and Farid see two men haggling over in the street?
   A. A torn blanket
   B. A baby's bottle
   C. A basket of fresh naan
   D. An artificial leg

2. What does Amir look for when he climbs the hill to the cemetery where he and Hassan used to play?
   A. The marking for where Hassan was buried
   B. The old story book they used to read
   C. The slingshot Hassan used to play with
   D. The carving on the tree

3. Even though it is really hot, what are all the soccer players wearing?
   A. Long robes
   B. Wool jackets
   C. Heavy head garmets
   D. Long pants

4. What happens at half-time during the soccer game?
   A. The crowd takes a break for afternoon prayer
   B. A popular musician plays patriotic music as people dance in the aisle
   C. Amir meets with the man who knows of Sohrab's whereabouts
   D. The Taliban stones two people to death

5. Why doesn't Farid go with Amir to meet with the man in white with the sunglasses to ask about Sohrab?
   A. He has another appointment.
   B. It is too dangerous.
   C. He owes the man money.
   D. He has other errands to run.

6. Why could Amir be arrested for treason?
   A. For not fighting with his fellow Muslims and leaving to live in America
   B. For talking to others about how great Afghanistan used to be with the old government
   C. For looking at members of the Taliban with disrespect
   D. For questioning the actions of the Taliban while in public

7. What does Sohrab do when he enters the room when Amir sees him for the first time?
   A. Carry a platter of meats to each guest
   B. Kiss each person in the room
   C. Sing
   D. Dance

8. Who is the man with the sunglasses?
   A. Rahim Khan
   B. Kamul
   C. Assef
   D. The manager of the orphanage

9. What does Amir have to do to "earn" Sohrab?
   A. Amir has to fight Assef.
   B. Amir has to move back to Afghanistan.
   C. Amir has to bring Assef $2000.00.
   D. Amir has to build an orphanage.

10. Why does Amir start laughing when he is in so much pain?
   A. He realizes that for the first time since the winter of 1975 he is at peace, even though he is getting severely beaten.
   B. He hits a breaking point from the pain where his mind and body begin to shut down. All he can do is laugh until he is almost hysterical and can no longer feel the pain.
   C. He cannot believe how things have worked out in his life. He can't help but laugh at the irony of the situation.
   D. He understands that this is the punishment he must receive in order to be cleared of his sins and live a peaceful afterlife, which makes him laugh at God's twisted sense of humor.

11. Describe how Amir is finally able to leave the room and get away to safety with Sohrab.

A. Amir is beaten so severely he goes into shock. The man from the Taliban thinks this comatose state is actually death, and leaves Amir to die in the room. Sohrab is left alone in the room and notices a faint breathing coming from Amir. He then waits until night to drag Amir's body outside where Farid is waiting with the car.

B. Amir gives up and allows the man to beat him to near death. The man from the Taliban gets angry that Amir is laughing at him and not fighting back and throws him out of the room to die. Farid sees this and hurries to take him to safety.

C. Sohrab finds a brass ball and shoots the man from the Taliban in the eye with his slingshot.

D. Sohrab takes a knife he had hidden in his waistband and stabs the man from the Taliban. This does not kill him but stuns him long enough for Amir to pull the knife out and stab him in the heart, killing him and allowing them to leave.

Assignment 9
Chapters 23-24

1. Describe some of Amir's most severe injuries.
   A. He has a collapsed lung, his liver is bleeding internally, he has a mild concussion, his right arm is broken in three places, several teeth are missing, his vision is permanently damaged in one eye, and his ankle has pins holding it together.
   B. Both of his legs are broken, he has several fractured ribs, he has stitches across the top portion of his scalp, four of his fingernails are gone, his eye is bruised, and he has several deep cuts.
   C. Both of his arms are broken, he has a severe laceration on this throat, one kidney has to be removed, his nose is fractured, he dislocated his shoulder, one ear was nearly ripped off, he has 77 stitches on the inside of his left leg, and he has bruises covering most of his body.
   D. His mouth is wired shut from a broken jaw, he has a ruptured spleen, several broken ribs, a punctured lung, a broken bone around his eye socket, several missing teeth, and many cuts.

2. What is the significance of Amir's injury to his lip?
   A. Amir has the same scar that Hassan had with his harelip.
   B. Amir has the same scar that Sohrab has, making them look like father and son.
   C. Amir will no longer be able to smile, just like Hassan did not smile in all those years he suffered from what happened after the kite tournament.
   D. Amir will no longer be able to speak normally, making him sound even less American when he returns home to the United States.

3. What happened to Rahim Khan?
   A. His was killed for talking back to the Taliban as they went from home to home looking for money and valuables to steal.
   B. He flew to America to spend his last days in a country he had longed to visit his entire life.
   C. He passed away from an advanced form of lung cancer.
   D. He left town when Amir did and left only a note and keys to a safety deposit box behind for Amir when he returned.

4. Why does Amir leave the hospital in Peshawar and go to Islamabad?
   A. The Taliban are looking for Amir so he is not safe in Peshawar.
   B. The hospital finds out Amir has been living in America and refuses to continue to treat him for free.
   C. The doctors are unable to perform the more complicated surgeries Amir requires.
   D. Amir has to get Sohrab to safety before the orphanage director comes looking for him.

5. Amir planned on leaving Sohrab with the Caldwell family in Pakistan. Why does Amir suddenly have to change his plans and become responsible for Sohrab?
   A. The Caldwell family already have fourteen orphans living with them. They are unable to take in another and send Sohrab away.
   B. The Caldwell family never existed. They were a lie Rahim told Amir to push him to go get Sohrab.
   C. The Caldwell family was deported from Afghanistan and sent back to America for interfering with national affairs.
   D. The Caldwell family was killed in a Taliban raid three days after Amir went to get Sohrab.

6. What does Amir give to Farid for helping him on his journey to find Sohrab?
   A. He gives him all the money Rahim left, a little over $2,000.
   B. He gives him the car they used for their travels and promises to send his children toys from America.
   C. He gives him and his family money for airfare to America to stay with him and his wife in San Francisco.
   D. He gives him a handshake and a sincere thanks for all his help.

7. Where does Sohrab go when he runs away?
   A. The crowded marketplace
   B. The large mosque
   C. The kite store
   D. The orphanage

8. Why is Sohrab scared to go with Amir to America?
   A. He is afraid that Amir will get tired of him or that Amir's wife won't like him.
   B. He is scared if he leaves his country his mother and father would be dishonored.
   C. He is afraid the kids in America will laugh at his accent and make fun of his Hazara looks.
   D. He is scared he will not learn English and will have no friends.

9. What does Amir discover at the American embassy when trying to get information about adopting Sohrab?
   A. The process will cost a lot of money to pay off various agencies involved.
   B. The process will be relatively easy as long as Sohrab gives his consent.
   C. The process will be pretty cheap and simple since no one pays much attention to Afghan children.
   D. The process will be nearly impossible.

10. What does Sohrab do at the hotel each night before bed?
    A. He thanks the manager for allowing them to stay another night.
    B. He takes a very long, hot bath.
    C. He watches a puppet show on TV.
    D. He drinks a glass of orange juice.

11. What suggestion does the immigration lawyer give to Amir as his best chance of getting Sohrab out of Afghanistan and into America?
    A. To travel first to Germany and then attempt to go to America since they would be leaving a more stable country
    B. To pay the $25,000 to the immigration officials to get him a permit to travel
    C. To purchase a fake ID that shows Sohrab is an America citizen
    D. To relinquish him to an orphanage and start the paperwork through a private adoption agency

12. What good news does Soraya give Amir?
    A. She finally got pregnant
    B. Her uncle is able to get Sohrab into the country immediately and without any problems
    C. She is coming to Afghanistan to visit Amir and Sohrab
    D. Her family came up with the money to bring Sohrab to America

13. What does Amir discover when he goes into the bathroom to talk to Sohrab?
    A. Sohrab is bleeding and unconscious in the tub.
    B. Sohrab is dancing and singing. He is overjoyed with the good news and Amir has never seen him to happy.
    C. Sohrab is smiling. Amir has not seen Sohrab smile since he met him.
    D. Sohrab is gone. He has run away again and Amir is worried he won't be able to find him.

Assignment 10
Chapter 25

1. What "bargain" does Amir make with God?
   A. He promises to convert others to the Muslim religion if God will get Sohrab to America safely.
   B. He promises to be a practicing Muslim if God will save Sohrab's life.
   C. He promises to volunteer and give back to the community if he will save Sohrab's life.
   D. He promises to donate money to the church if God will get Sohrab to America safely.

2. What did Sohrab do to himself?
   A. He used a laundry line to hang himself to try to commit suicide.
   B. He tried to drown himself in the tub to commit suicide.
   C. He used Amir's razor blade to try to commit suicide.
   D. He electrocuted himself to try to commit suicide.

3. What does Sohrab say he wants?
   A. To go to America
   B. To stay in Afghanistan
   C. His slingshot
   D. His old life back

4. What does Sohrab's new room in America look like?
   A. It is decorated with soccer gear. There is a goal set up on one end of the room and several posters of Afghan soccer players on the wall.
   B. It is decorated with colorful kites. There is also a growing chart on the wall and a basket overflowing with toys.
   C. It is decorated with famous American landmarks. There is a set of bunk beds and a closet full of brand new clothes.
   D. It is decorated with cars. There is a bed frame shaped like a sports car and a rug that looks like a map on the floor for him to play cars on.

5. In what way does Amir stand up to the General for the first time?
   A. The General tells Amir it was a mistake to bring Sohrab to America. Amir asks him to leave their home until he can begin to act more like a loving grandfather.
   B. The General tells Soraya that she should quit her job and stay home with Sohrab. Amir tells him that Soraya is a talented teacher and will work as long as she desires.
   C. The General calls Sohrab a Hazara boy, and Amir tells him never to use that term in his presence again.
   D. The General plays too roughly with Sohrab, making him cry. Amir asks him to leave and give Sohrab some space.

6. Describe how Sohrab acts once in America.
   A. He is making progress in learning English and has made a few friends in the neighborhood.
   B. He is silent and sleeps a lot.
   C. He is struggling to learn English but enjoys seeing California and experiencing new things.
   D. He is talkative when it is just Amir, but hasn't warmed up to strangers.

7. What significant historical event happens a few months after Amir returns to America?
   A. President Bush stops allowing immigrants into the United States.
   B. George W. Bush is elected President of the United States.
   C. The twin towers in New York City fall on September 11, 2001.
   D. China and France become allies with Afghanistan.

8. With what project does Amir get involved?
   A. Raising money for a hospital on the Afghanistan/Pakistan border
   B. Helping families in America adopt children in war-torn countries
   C. Working to develop a democratic government in Afghanistan
   D. Sending clothes and toys to orphanages in Afghanistan

9. What celebration do Amir and his family attend?
   A. The baptism of Sohrab
   B. The Ramadan
   C. The feast for Eid ul-Fitr
   D. The Afghan New Year's Day

10. What does Amir buy at the celebration Amir and his hamily attend?
    A. A bottle of fine Afghan wine
    B. A kite
    C. A guitar
    D. A slingshot

11. What happens at the celebration Amir and his family attend that makes Sohrab smile?
    A. He tries a glass of wine, and it makes him remember feasting with his father.
    B. He sees a framed picture of Amir and Hassan along with their favorite children's book.
    C. He meets another orphan from Afghanistan who has experienced many of the same conditions he did.
    D. He flies a kite with Amir. The two fight another kite and win.

ANSWER KEY: STUDY QUESTIONS *The Kite Runner*

	1	2	3	4	5	6	7	8	9	10
1	D	B	C	A	A	C	C	D	D	B
2	C	D	D	A	A	B	A	D	A	C
3	B	B	A	C	A	A	A	D	D	D
4	A	A	B	B	C	A	C	D	A	B
5	A	B	C	B	A	B	A	B	B	C
6	A	D	A	A	B	D	D	A	A	B
7	B	C	B	A	D	B	A	D	B	C
8	A	A	D	C	B	B	B	C	A	A
9	B	C	C	B	C	B	A	A	D	D
10	C	A	B	B	B	D	A	A	B	B
11	C	D	A	C	D	B	A	C	D	D
12	C	A	B	D	D	B	D		B	
13		D	C		B	D	C		A	

VOCABULARY WORKSHEETS

VOCABULARY ASSIGNMENT 1 *The Kite Runner*

Part I: Using Prior Knowledge and Contextual Clues

Below are the sentences in which the vocabulary words appear in the text. Read the sentence. Use any clues you can find in the sentence combined with your prior knowledge, and write what you think the underlined words mean on the lines provided.

1. Everyone agreed that my father, my Baba, had built the most beautiful house in the Wazir Akbar Khan district, a new and affluent neighborhood in the northern part of Kabul.

   ____

2. People had raised their eyebrows when Ali, a man who had memorized the Koran, married Sanaubar, a woman nineteen years younger, a beautiful but notoriously unscrupulous woman who lived up to her dishonorable reputation.

   ____

3. People had raised their eyebrows when Ali, a man who had memorized the Koran, married Sanaubar, a woman nineteen years younger, a beautiful but notoriously unscrupulous woman who lived up to her dishonorable reputation.

   ____

4. I have heard that Sanaubar's suggestive stride and oscillating hips sent men to reveries of infidelity.

   ____

5. But polio had left Ali with a twisted, atrophied right leg that was sallow skin over bone with little in between except a paper-thin layer of muscle.

   ____

6. It said the Hazaras had tried to rise against the Pashtuns in the nineteenth century, but the Pashtuns had "quelled them with unspeakable violence."

   ____

7. As confided to a neighbor's servant by the garrulous midwife, who had then in turn told anyone who would listen, Sanaubar had taken one glance at the baby in Ali's arms, seen the cleft lip, and barked with bitter laughter.

   ____

8. They would leave with the bag tucked out of sight, sometimes drawing furtive, disapproving glances from those who knew about the store's reputation for such transactions.

   ____

9. I cried all the way back home. I remember how Baba's hands clenched around the steering wheel. Clenched and unclenched. Mostly, I will never forget Baba's valiant efforts to conceal the disgusted look on his face as he drove in silence.

   ____

10. Baba nodded and gave a thin smile that conveyed little more than <u>feigned</u> interest.

____

The Kite Runner Vocabulary Worksheet Assignment 1 Continued

Part II: Determining the Meaning -- Match the vocabulary words to their dictionary definitions.

____ 1.	AFFLUENT	A.	Daydreams
____ 2.	NOTORIOUSLY	B.	Pacified: quieted or suppressed
____ 3.	UNSCRUPULOUS	C.	Having no conscience or principles; oblivious to what is right or honorable
____ 4.	REVERIES	D.	Not real; pretended
____ 5.	ATROPHIED	E.	Wasted; withered; shriveled
____ 6.	QUELLED	F.	Boldly courageous; brave
____ 7.	GARRULOUS	G.	Secret; sly; shifty
____ 8.	FURTIVE	H.	Excessively talkative in a rambling, roundabout manner, especially about trivial matters
____ 9.	VALIANT	I.	Generously supplied with money, property, or possessions; prosperous or rich
____ 10.	FEIGNED	J.	Known widely and usually unfavorably known

VOCABULARY ASSIGNMENT 2 *The Kite Runner*

Part I: Using Prior Knowledge and Contextual Clues

Below are the sentences in which the vocabulary words appear in the text. Read the sentence. Use any clues you can find in the sentence combined with your prior knowledge, and write what you think the underlined words mean on the lines provided.

1. Hassan shrugged. To an outsider, he didn't look scared. But Hassan's face was my earliest memory and I knew all of its subtle nuances, knew each and every twitch and flicker that ever rippled across it.

   ____

2. Neither one of us said much of anything as we walked home in trepidation, certain that Assef and his friends would ambush us every time we turned a corner.

   ____

3. We both looked to Ali, but of course with him you could never tell. His face was impassive as ever, though something sober had melted into his eyes.

   ____

4. The immensely popular Ahmad Zahir had revolutionized Afghan music and outraged the purists by adding electric guitars, drums, and horns to the traditional table and harmonium; on stage or at parties, he shirked the austere and nearly morose stance of older singers and actually smiled when he sang--sometimes at women.

   ____

5. The immensely popular Ahmad Zahir had revolutionized Afghan music and outraged the purists by adding electric guitars, drums, and horns to the traditional table and harmonium; on stage or at parties, he shirked the austere and nearly morose stance of older singers and actually smiled when he sang--sometimes at women.

   ____

6. Then he smiled his Hassan smile and disappeared around the corner. The next time I saw him smile unabashedly like that was twenty-six years later, in a faded Polaroid photograph.

   ____

7. I watch because of that look of acceptance in the animal's eyes. Absurdly, I imagine the animal understands. I image the animal sees that its imminent demise is for a higher purpose.

   ____

8. I watch because of that look of acceptance in the animal's eyes. Absurdly, I imagine the animal understands. I imagine the animal sees that its imminent demise is for a higher purpose.

   ____

9. Did he know I knew? And if he knew, then what would I see if I did look in his eyes? Blame? Indignation? Or, God forbid, what I feared most: guileless devotion? That, most of all, I couldn't bear to see.

    ____

10. Did he know I knew? And if he knew, then what would I see if I did look in his eyes? Blame? Indignation? Or, God forbid, what I feared most: guileless devotion? That, most of all, I couldn't bear to see.

    ____

The Kite Runner Vocabulary Worksheet Assignment 2 Continued

Part II: Determining the Meaning -- Match the vocabulary words to their dictionary definitions.

____ 1.	NUANCES	A.	Grave; strict; solemn; serious
____ 2.	TREPIDATION	B.	Likely to occur at any moment; impending
____ 3.	IMPASSIVE	C.	Sincere; honest; straightforward
____ 4.	AUSTERE	D.	Anger aroused by something unjust, mean, or unworthy
____ 5.	MOROSE	E.	Subtle differences or distinctions in expression, meaning, or response
____ 6.	UNABASHEDLY	F.	A state of alarm or dread; apprehension
____ 7.	IMMINENT	G.	Without emotion; unmoved
____ 8.	DEMISE	H.	Not concealed or disguised; obviously
____ 9.	INDIGNATION	I.	Death or decline
____ 10.	GUILELESS	J.	Melancholy; gloomy

VOCABULARY ASSIGNMENT 3 *The Kite Runner*

Part I: Using Prior Knowledge and Contextual Clues

Below are the sentences in which the vocabulary words appear in the text. Read the sentence. Use any clues you can find in the sentence combined with your prior knowledge, and write what you think the underlined words mean on the lines provided.

1. We'd actually deceived ourselves into thinking that a toy made of tissue paper, glue, and bamboo could somehow close the chasm between us.

   ____

2. To my dismay, Hassan kept trying to rekindle things between us.

   ____

3. Hassan milled about the periphery of my life after that. I made sure our paths crossed as little as possible, planned my day that way.

   ____

4. Students with new notebooks and sharpened pencils in hand ambled about the courtyard, kicking up dust, chatting in groups, waiting for the class captain's whistles.

   ____

5. I turned thirteen that summer of 1976, Afghanistan's next to last summer of peace and anonymity.

   ____

6. On the surface, he was the embodiment of every parent's dream, a strong, tall, well-dressed and well-mannered boy with talent and striking looks, not to mention the wit to joke with an adult. But to me, his eyes betrayed him. When I looked into them, the facade faltered, revealed a glimpse of the madness hiding behind them.

   ____

7. On the surface, he was the embodiment of every parent's dream, a strong, tall, well-dressed and well-mannered boy with talent and striking looks, not to mention the wit to joke with an adult. But to me, his eyes betrayed him. When I looked into them, the facade faltered, revealed a glimpse of the madness hiding behind them.

   ____

8. Baba stood up, a sheen of grief across his face.

   ____

9. His mouth twitched and, for a moment, I though I saw a grimace. That was when I understood the depth of the pain I had caused, the blackness of the grief I had brought onto everyone, that not even Ali's paralyzed face could mask his sorrow.

   ____

The Kite Runner Vocabulary Worksheet Assignment 3 Continued

Part II: Determining the Meaning -- Match the vocabulary words to their dictionary definitions.

____ 1.	CHASM	A.	Agitation; perturbation; alarm
____ 2.	DISMAY	B.	A facial expression that indicates disapproval or pain
____ 3.	PERIPHERY	C.	A pronounced difference of opinion, interests, or loyalty
____ 4.	AMBLED	D.	Moved with a slow, easy walk; strolled
____ 5.	ANONYMITY	E.	The quality or state of being unknown or unacknowledged
____ 6.	EMBODIMENT	F.	An artificial or deceptive front
____ 7.	FACADE	G.	Glistening brightness; radiance
____ 8.	SHEEN	H.	To exemplify in concrete form
____ 9.	GRIMACE	I.	The edge or outskirts

VOCABULARY ASSIGNMENT 4 *The Kite Runner*

Part I: Using Prior Knowledge and Contextual Clues

Below are the sentences in which the vocabulary words appear in the text. Read the sentence. Use any clues you can find in the sentence combined with your prior knowledge, and write what you think the underlined words mean on the lines provided.

1. Baba never said so, but I knew he saw my car sickness as yet another of my array of weakness--I saw it on his embarrassed face the couple of times my stomach had clenched so badly I moaned.

   ____

2. Karim was a people smuggleler--it was a pretty lucrative business then, driving people out of Shorawi-occupied Kabul to the relative safety of Pakistan.

   ____

3. Mahipar--which means "Flying Fish"--was a high summit with a precipitous drop overlooking the hydro plant the Germans had built for Afghanistan back in 1967.

   ____

4. "War doesn't negate decency. It demands it, even more than in times of peace."

   ____

5. He gave the younger officer the rueful look of a father exasperated with his misbehaving son.

   ____

6. He gave the younger officer the rueful look of a father exasperated with his misbehaving son.

   ____

7. The stench of something dank, like mildew, bludgeoned my nostrils the moment Karim opened the door that led down the creaky steps to the basement.

   ____

8. And that was how Baba ended those humiliating food stamp moments at the cash register and alleviated one of his greatest fears: that an Afghan would see him buying food with charity money.

   ____

9. "Well, people need stories to divert them at difficult times like this."

   ____

10. "You know me," Baba said, inching the bus along the queue exiting the flea market.

    ____

The Kite Runner Vocabulary Worksheet Assignment 4 Continued

Part II: Determining the Meaning -- Match the vocabulary words to their dictionary definitions.

____ 1.	ARRAY	A. A file or line, especially of people waiting in turn
____ 2.	LUCRATIVE	B. An impressively large number
____ 3.	PRECIPITOUS	C. Profitable; moneymaking
____ 4.	NEGATE	D. To make ineffective or invalid; nullify
____ 5.	RUEFUL	E. Made easier to endure; lessened
____ 6.	EXASPERATED	F. Causing sorrow or pity; deplorable; mournful
____ 7.	BLUDGEONED	G. Hit or overcame
____ 8.	ALLEVIATED	H. To distract from serious occupation; entertain or amuse
____ 9.	DIVERT	I. Extremely steep
____ 10.	QUEUE	J. Made very angry or impatient; annoyed greatly

VOCABULARY ASSIGNMENT 5 *The Kite Runner*

Part I: Using Prior Knowledge and Contextual Clues

Below are the sentences in which the vocabulary words appear in the text. Read the sentence. Use any clues you can find in the sentence combined with your prior knowledge, and write what you think the underlined words mean on the lines provided.

1. When I was older, I read in my poetry books that *yelda* was the starless night tormented lovers kept vigil, enduring the endless dark, waiting for the sun to rise and bring with it their loved one.

    ____

2. Honor and pride. The tenets of Pashtun men. Especially when it came to the chastity of a wife. Or a daughter.

    ____

3. But he wouldn't say more--Baba knew how lethal idle talk could prove to a young woman's prospects of marrying well. Afghan men, especially those from reputable families, were fickle creatures. A whisper here, an insinuation there, and they fled like startled birds.

    ____

4. I could never read the thoughts in the general's eyes, but I knew this much about his wife: If I was going to have an adversary in this--whatever *this* was--it would not be her.

    ____

5. "There is chemotherapy, of course," he said. "But it would only be palliative."

    ____

6. But there was a new reticence to Khanum Taheri's demeanor. A reticence broken only by her secret, droopy smiles and the furtive, apologetic looks she cast my way when the general's attention was engaged elsewhere.

    ____

7. Soraya joined me at San Jose State the following year and enrolled, to her father's chagrin, in the teaching track.

    ____

8. The idea of fatherhood unleashed a swirl of emotions in me. I found it frightening, invigorating, daunting, and exhilarating all at the same time.

    ____

9. We used the advance I had received for my novel to pay for it. IVF proved lengthy, meticulous, frustrating, and ultimately unsuccessful.

    ____

10. We'd talked at home about adoption. Soraya was ambivalent at best.

    ____

The Kite Runner Vocabulary Worksheet Assignment 5 Continued

Part II: Determining the Meaning -- Match the vocabulary words to their dictionary definitions.

____ 1.	VIGIL	A.	A watch kept during normal sleeping hours
____ 2.	TENETS	B.	Extremely careful and precise; paying great attention to details
____ 3.	INSINUATION	C.	A feeling of vexation, marked by disappointment or humiliation
____ 4.	ADVERSARY	D.	An indirect or covert suggestion or hint especially of a derogatory nature
____ 5.	PALLIATIVE	E.	Opinions, doctrines, or principles held as being true by a person or especially by an organization
____ 6.	RETICENCE	F.	Relieving or soothing the symptoms of a disease or disorder without affecting a cure
____ 7.	CHAGRIN	G.	Discouraging through fear
____ 8.	DAUNTING	H.	State of being reluctant or reserved
____ 9.	METICULOUS	I.	Opponent; enemy
____ 10.	AMBIVALENT	J.	Uncertain or unable to decide about what course to follow

VOCABULARY ASSIGNMENT 6 *The Kite Runner*

Part I: Using Prior Knowledge and Contextual Clues

Below are the sentences in which the vocabulary words appear in the text. Read the sentence. Use any clues you can find in the sentence combined with your prior knowledge, and write what you think the underlined words mean on the lines provided.

1. Our lovemaking was still good, at times better than good, but some nights all I'd feel was a relief to be done with it, to be free to drift away and forget, at least for a while, about the futility of what we'd just done.

   ____

2. My driver, a chain-smoking, sweaty little man who introduced himself as Gholam, drove nonchalantly and recklessly, averting collisions by the thinnest of margins, all without so much as a pause in the incessant stream of words spewing from his mouth.

   ____

3. My driver, a chain-smoking, sweaty little man who introduced himself as Gholam, drove nonchalantly and recklessly, averting collisions by the thinnest of margins, all without so much as a pause in the incessant stream of words spewing from his mouth.

   ____

4. My driver, a chain-smoking, sweaty little man who introduced himself as Gholam, drove nonchalantly and recklessly, averting collisions by the thinnest of margins, all without so much as a pause in the incessant stream of words spewing from his mouth.

   ____

5. But the aptness of the cliched saying is overshadowed by the nature of the saying as a cliche.

   ____

6. But I am not surrendering to fate here, I am being pragmatic.

   ____

7. Other than that, he had those same narrow green eyes, that scar on his upper lip, that round face, that affable smile.

   ____

8. Sunlight slanted in from the left, casting a shadow on half of his rotund face. He was squinting and smiling at the camera, showing a pair of missing front teeth. Even in this blurry Polaroid, the man in the *chapan* exuded a sense of self-assuredness, or ease.

   ____

9. Sunlight slanted in from the left, casting a shadow on half of his rotund face. He was squinting and smiling at the camera, showing a pair of missing front teeth. Even in this blurry Polaroid, the man in the *chapan* exuded a sense of self-assuredness, or ease.

   ____

10. Hassan slumps to the asphalt, his life of unrequited loyalty drifting from him like the windblown kites he used to chase.

____

The Kite Runner Vocabulary Worksheet Assignment 6 Continued

Part II: Determining the Meaning -- Match the vocabulary words to their dictionary definitions.

____ 1.	FUTILITY	A.	Preventing something from occurring
____ 2.	NONCHALANTLY	B.	Characterized by having no useful result; uselessness
____ 3.	AVERTING	C.	Dealing or concerned with facts or actual occurrences; practical
____ 4.	INCESSANT	D.	Continuing without interruption; ceaseless; unending
____ 5.	APTNESS	E.	Pleasantly easy to approach and to talk to; friendly; cordial; warmly polite
____ 6.	PRAGMATIC	F.	To project or display; radiate
____ 7.	AFFABLE	G.	Coolly unconcerned, indifferent, or unexcited manner; casually
____ 8.	ROTUND	H.	Round in shape; plump; fat
____ 9.	EXUDED	I.	Degree to which something is appropriate
____ 10.	UNREQUITED	J.	Not returned or reciprocated

VOCABULARY ASSIGNMENT 7 *The Kite Runner*

Part I: Using Prior Knowledge and Contextual Clues

Below are the sentences in which the vocabulary words appear in the text. Read the sentence. Use any clues you can find in the sentence combined with your prior knowledge, and write what you think the underlined words mean on the lines provided.

1. And with that came this realization: that Rahim Khan had summoned me here to atone not just for my sins but for Baba's too.

   ____

2. I wished Rahim Khan hadn't called me. I wished he had let me live on in my oblivion.

   ____

3. Something inside my stomach churned and twisted. Farid, my driver, threw me a cold glance. There was no empathy in his eyes.

   ____

4. The arid, imposing mountains sat along deep gorges and soared to jagged peaks.

   ____

5. "Old *watani* trick, no need for fancy medicine," he said. His tone bordered on the surly.

   ____

6. Pines trees flanked the road, fewer than I remembered and many of them bare, but it was good to see trees again after the arduous drive through the Khyber Pass.

   ____

7. The young woman stepped out of the way, eyeing me a little apprehensively as I followed Farid into the small house.

   ____

8. "What brings them *all* back to Afghanistan, dear brother?" Farid said, speaking to Wahid but fixing me with a contemptuous gaze.

   ____

9. "They drive around looking. Looking and hoping that someone will provoke them. Sooner or later, someone always obliges."

   ____

10. He hurriedly slipped the money in his waist, his lone eye darting side to side. "A world of thanks for your benevolence, Agha sahib."

    ____

The Kite Runner Vocabulary Worksheet Assignment 7 Continued

Part II: Determining the Meaning -- Match the vocabulary words to their dictionary definitions.

____ 1.	ATONE	A.	Does a service or favor for
____ 2.	OBLIVION	B.	Understanding of another's situation, feelings, and motives
____ 3.	EMPATHY	C.	Requiring great exertion; laborious; difficult
____ 4.	ARID	D.	The state of being completely forgotten or unknown
____ 5.	SURLY	E.	An inclination to perform kind, charitable acts
____ 6.	ARDUOUS	F.	To make amends, as for a sin or fault
____ 7.	APPREHENSIVELY	G.	Showing unease or fearfulness about something that might happen
____ 8.	CONTEMPTUOUS	H.	Being without moisture; extremely dry; parched
____ 9.	OBLIGES	I.	Rude or bad-tempered; unfriendly or hostile
____ 10.	BENEVOLENCE	J.	Showing or expressing contempt or disdain; scornful

VOCABULARY ASSIGNMENT 8 *The Kite Runner*

Part I: Using Prior Knowledge and Contextual Clues

Below are the sentences in which the vocabulary words appear in the text. Read the sentence. Use any clues you can find in the sentence combined with your prior knowledge, and write what you think the underlined words mean on the lines provided.

1. The windows to the living room, the foyer, and the upstairs guest bathroom were broken, patched haphazardly with sheets of clear plastic or wooden boards nailed across the frames.

   ____

2. He charged me $75, an unthinkable price given the run-down appearance of the place, but I didn't mind. Exploitation to finance a beach house in Hawaii was one thing. Doing it to feed your kids was another.

   ____

3. I rang the bell but no buzz came--still no electricity--and I had to pound on the doors. A moment later, I heard terse voices from the other side and a pair of men toting Kalashnikovs answered the door.

   ____

4. Nothing wrong with cowardice as long as it comes with prudence. But when a coward stops remembering who he is...God help him.

   ____

5. "You don't know the meaning of the word 'liberating' until you've done that, stood in a roomful of targets, let the bullets fly, free of guilt and remorse, knowing you are virtuous, good, and decent. Knowing you're doing God's work."

   ____

6. The two guards whistled and laughed. The Talib in white was tilting his head back and forth with the music, his mouth half-open in a leer.

   ____

7. I tried to take a breath and couldn't. I tried to blink and couldn't. The moment felt surreal--no, not surreal, absurd--it had knocked the breath out of me, brought the world around me to a standstill.

   ____

8. My past was like that, always turning up. His name rose from the deep and I didn't want to say it, as if uttering it might conjure him. But he was already here, in the flesh, sitting less than ten feet from me, after all these years.

   ____

9. "Well, as you may remember, I wasn't much of a religious type. But one day I had an epiphany. I had it in jail. Do you want to hear?"

   ____

10. I was on the ground laughing, Assef straddling my chest, his face a mask of lunacy, framed by snarls of his hair swaying inches from my face.

____

The Kite Runner Vocabulary Worksheet Assignment 8 Continued

Part II: Determining the Meaning -- Match the vocabulary words to their dictionary definitions.

____ 1. HAPHAZARDLY	A.	Deep and painful regret for wrongdoing
____ 2. EXPLOITATION	B.	Great or wild foolishness; insanity
____ 3. TERSE	C.	Brief and to the point
____ 4. PRUDENCE	D.	Caution with regard to practical matters; regard for one's own interests
____ 5. REMORSE	E.	Having the disorienting, hallucinatory quality of a dream; seeming unreal; fantastic
____ 6. LEER	F.	To look with a sidelong glance, especially with sexual desire or sly and malicious intent
____ 7. SURREAL	G.	The act of employing to the greatest possible advantage
____ 8. CONJURE	H.	To call or bring into existence by or as if by magic
____ 9. EPIPHANY	I.	In a random manner; without care
____ 10. LUNACY	J.	A sudden perception of or insight into the reality or essential meaning of something, usually initiated by some simple or commonplace occurrence or experience

VOCABULARY ASSIGNMENT 9 *The Kite Runner*

Part I: Using Prior Knowledge and Contextual Clues

Below are the sentences in which the vocabulary words appear in the text. Read the sentence. Use any clues you can find in the sentence combined with your prior knowledge, and write what you think the underlined words mean on the lines provided.

1. You had a right to know. So did Hassan. I know it doesn't absolve anyone of anything, but the Kabul we lived in in those days was a strange world, one in which some things mattered more than truth.

   ____

2. So he took it out on you instead--Amir, the socially legitimate half, the half that represented the riches he had inherited and the sin-with-impunity privileges that came with them.

   ____

3. Sometimes, I think everything he did, feeding the poor on the streets, building the orphanage, giving money to friends in need, it was all his way of redeeming himself. And that, I believe, is what true redemption is, Amir jan, when guilt leads to good.

   ____

4. "My boys are young, but they are very shrewd. They know how to take care of their mothers and sisters."

   ____

5. Now, as the boy's pain soaked through my shirt, I saw that a kinship had taken root between us too. What had happened in that room with Assef had irrevocably bound us.

   ____

6. I had found the boy in squalid conditions, wasting away in an orphanage.

   ____

7. In truth, I didn't remember the last time I had laid my forehead to the ground in prayer. Then I did remember: the day Dr. Armani gave Baba his prognosis.

   ____

8. "I'm familiar with the version of the situation you gave Mr. Andrews," he said. His cheeks dimpled with a coy smile. He turned to Sohrab. "This must be the young man who's causing all the trouble," he said in Farsi.

   ____

9. "Well, it's like this. In the aftermath of a disaster, whether it be natural or man-made--and the Taliban are a disaster, Amir, believe me--it's always difficult to ascertain that a child is an orphan."

   ____

10. "Finally, adoption agencies routinely send staff members to evaluate the child's milieu, and no reasonable agency is going to send an agent to Afghanistan."

____

The Kite Runner Vocabulary Worksheet Assignment 9 Continued

Part II: Determining the Meaning -- Match the vocabulary words to their dictionary definitions.

____ 1.	ABSOLVE	A.	Freed from guilt or blame
____ 2.	IMPUNITY	B.	Affectedly modest or shy especially in a playful or provocative way
____ 3.	REDEMPTION	C.	An environment or a setting; surroundings
____ 4.	SHREWD	D.	Foul and repulsive, as from lack of care or cleanliness; neglected and filthy
____ 5.	IRREVOCABLY	E.	A prediction of the probable course and outcome of a disease
____ 6.	SQUALID	F.	To make up for; make amends for
____ 7.	PROGNOSIS	G.	To find out for certain
____ 8.	COY	H.	Characterized by keen awareness, sharp intelligence, and often a sense of the practical
____ 9.	ASCERTAIN	I.	Not to be revoked or recalled; unable to be repealed or annulled; unalterable
____ 10.	MILIEU	J.	Exemption from punishment, penalty, or harm

VOCABULARY ASSIGNMENT 10 *The Kite Runner*

Part I: Using Prior Knowledge and Contextual Clues

Below are the sentences in which the vocabulary words appear in the text. Read the sentence. Use any clues you can find in the sentence combined with your prior knowledge, and write what you think the underlined words mean on the lines provided.

1. I bow to the west and kiss the ground and promise that I will do *zakat,* I will do *namaz,* I will fast during Ramadan and when Ramadan has passed I will go on fasting, I will commit to memory every last word of His holy book, and I will set on a pilgrimage to that sweltering city in the desert and bow before the Ka'bah too.

   ____

2. In the daytime, the hospital was a maze of teeming, angled hallways, a blur of blazing-white overhead fluorescence.

   ____

3. Sohrab was under twenty-four-hours-a-day suicide watch. Hospital protocol, Dr. Nawaz had informed me.

   ____

4. So what I took as a yes from him was in actuality more of a quiet surrender, not so much an acceptance as an act of relinquishment by one too weary to decide, and far too tired to believe.

   ____

5. I had been the entitled half, the society-approved, legitimate half, the unwitting embodiment of Baba's guilt.

   ____

6. It would be erroneous to say Sohrab was quiet. Quiet is peace. Tranquility. Quiet is turning down the VOLUME knob on life. Silence is pushing the OFF button. Shutting it down. All of it.

   ____

7. With time, the queries about our adopted--and decidedly eccentric--little boy had mercifully ceased, and, considering how tactless Afghan queries can be sometimes, that was a considerable relief.

   ____

8. With time, the queries about our adopted--and decidedly eccentric--little boy had mercifully ceased, and, considering how tactless Afghan queries can be sometimes, that was a considerable relief.

   ____

9. The novelty had worn off. Like dull wallpaper, Sohrab had blended into the background.

   ____

10. Behind us, kids were scampering, and a <u>melee</u> of screaming kite runners was chasing the loose kite drifting high above the trees.

____

The Kite Runner Vocabulary Worksheet Assignment 10 Continued

Part II: Determining the Meaning -- Match the vocabulary words to their dictionary definitions.

____ 1. PILGRIMAGE	A.	Unintentional; accidental; not knowing; unaware
____ 2. TEEMING	B.	Departing from a recognized, conventional, or established norm
____ 3. PROTOCOL	C.	Containing error; mistaken; incorrect; wrong
____ 4. RELINQUISHMENT	D.	A code of correct conduct
____ 5. UNWITTING	E.	Something unique or new
____ 6. ERRONEOUS	F.	Questions; inquiries
____ 7. QUERIES	G.	A journey, especially a long one, made to some sacred place as an act of religious devotion
____ 8. ECCENTRIC	H.	Abounding or swarming with something, as with people
____ 9. NOVELTY	I.	Giving up; surrendering
____ 10. MELEE	J.	A confused hand-to-hand fight or struggle among several people

VOCABULARY ANSWER KEY - *The Kite Runner*

	1	2	3	4	5	6	7	8	9	10
1	I	E	C	B	A	B	F	I	A	G
2	J	F	A	C	E	G	D	G	J	H
3	C	G	I	I	D	A	B	C	F	D
4	A	A	D	D	I	D	H	D	H	I
5	E	J	E	F	F	I	I	A	I	A
6	B	H	H	J	H	C	C	F	D	C
7	H	B	F	G	C	E	G	E	E	F
8	G	I	G	E	G	H	J	H	B	B
9	F	D	B	H	B	F	A	J	G	E
10	D	C		A	J	J	E	B	C	J

DAILY LESSONS

LESSON ONE

Objectives

To learn background information about Afghanistan

Activity

Before students read *The Kite Runner*, they should be aware of some important background information about Afghanistan, the Soviet invasion, and the Taliban.

The History Channel DVD on The Taliban (available from www.tpet.com, The History Channel, Amazon.com, or other sources) is a 50-minute presentation which gives a good summary of recent Afghan history and culture, especially the Soviet invasion and the rise of the Taliban (which are important events in the Kite Runner story).

Use this class time to show the Taliban DVD.

As an alternative (or in addition to the DVD), you could check out a laptop and projector and use online resources to cover these topics. A list of websites with useful information is listed below to help you get started. *At the publication date of this LitPlan, these web addresses are valid; they may, over time, change. If these are not working at the time you are using this LitPlan, do an Internet search for each of the topics above to find current web sites.*

- PBS America at a Crossroads: Interactive timeline for countries in the Middle East http://www.pbs.org/weta/crossroads/?campaign=pbshomefeatures_1_americaatacrossroads_2007-04-19

-CNN Afghanistan under the Taliban: Videos, sound clips, and articles on the Taliban rule in Afghanistan http://www.cnn.com/SPECIALS/2001/taliban/

-PBS Islam: Empire of Faith: Interactive pages outlining the fundamentals of the Islamic religion http://www.pbs.org/empires/islam/index.html

-Wikipedia Hazara People: Information on the Hazara people of Afghanistan http://en.wikipedia.org/wiki/Hazara_people

-Wikipedia Pashtun People: Information on the Pashtun people of Afghanistan http://en.wikipedia.org/wiki/Pashtun

LESSON TWO

Objectives

1. To introduce *The Kite Runner* unit
2. To distribute books, study questions, and other related materials
3. To preview the vocabulary and study questions for Assignment 1
4. To introduce the project assignment for this unit
5. To read Assignment 1

Activity #1
Ask students to take out a sheet of paper and brainstorm a list of things that come to mind when they hear the word Afghanistan. Tell students to think about the culture, religion, geography, government, and people that live in this country. Instruct students to write down anything that comes to mind.

After giving students 5-10 minutes to compile their lists, come together as a class and create a list of things Americans typically associate with Afghanistan on the board. Be sure to include both the positive and the negative comments that students wrote.

Activity #2
Explain to students that while reading the novel they will encounter words from the Afghan language, information about the culture and traditions, and information about the history of the country. Tell students that they will be documenting this information mentioned in the novel and creating a scrapbook exploring and celebrating the Afghan culture. Distribute the project requirement sheets and discuss them with your students.

Activity #3
Distribute the materials students will use in this unit. Explain in detail how students are to use these materials.

Study Guides Students should read the study guide questions for each reading assignment prior to beginning the reading assignment to get a feeling for what events and ideas are important in the section they are about to read. After reading the section, students will (as a class or individually) answer the questions to review the important events and ideas from that section of the book. Students should keep the study guides as study materials for the unit test. **Review the study questions for Assignment 1 while you're looking at the study guides.**

Vocabulary Prior to each reading assignment, students will do vocabulary work related to the section of the book they are about to read. Following the completion of the reading of the book, there will be a vocabulary review of all the words used in the vocabulary assignments. Students should keep their vocabulary work as study materials for the unit test. **Do Assignment 1 together orally to show students how to do the vocabulary worksheets.**

Reading Assignment Sheet You need to fill in the reading assignment sheet to let students know by when their reading has to be completed. You can either write the assignment sheet up on a side blackboard or bulletin board and leave it there for students to see each day, or you can make copies for each student to have. In either case, you should advise students to become very familiar with the reading assignments so they know what is expected of them.

Extra Activities Center The Unit Resource Materials portion of this LitPlan contains suggested topics for an extra library of related books and articles in your classroom, as well as crossword and word search puzzles. Make an extra activities center in your room where you will keep these materials for students to use. (Bring the books and articles in from the library and keep several copies of the puzzles on hand.) Explain to students that these materials are available for use when they finish reading assignments or other class work early.

Non-fiction Assignment Sheet Explain to students that they each are to read at least one non-fiction piece from the in-class library at some time during the unit. Students will fill out a Non-fiction Assignment Sheet after completing the reading to help you (the teacher) evaluate their reading experiences and to help the students think about and evaluate their own reading experiences.

Books Each school has its own rules and regulations regarding student use of school books. Advise students of the procedures that are normal for your school. Preview the book. Look at the covers, frontmatter, and index.

Activity #5
Tell students that they should read Assignment 1 prior to the next class period. Give them the remainder of this class (if time remains) to complete this assignment.

CULTURE APPRECIATION SCRAPBOOK PROJECT ASSIGNMENT *The Kite Runner*

PROMPT

The goal of this assignment is to find an appreciation for the Afghanistan culture and display your findings in a way that will help others to see the beauty of this country and its people. While reading *The Kite Runner* you will encounter many beliefs, customs, practices, and historical bits of information regarding Afghanistan. You should find several aspects of their culture that are unique and different from your own. You will then explore these differences through additional research and work to build an attractive, creative scrapbook covering a wide array of topics related to the Afghan culture.

PREWRITING

The best way to begin your project is to document words and cultural references you find while reading *The Kite Runner.* You may want to keep sticky notes or page flags with you while reading so you may easily refer back to the pages you need when working on your project. After each reading assignment is complete, review your notations and decide what you want to include in your project. You may also use notes or information from additional research.

Sometimes the author will provide you with all the information you need to understand a specific aspect of the Afghan culture, while other times you will need to seek additional resources.

To keep from falling behind in your project, try to conduct research, collect quotations, and find pictures/graphics/artwork for the topics you read about at the end of each reading assignment. Things you might want to pay attention to include: words and their meanings from the Afghan language, historical events, religious beliefs and customs, common foods, enjoyable pastimes and hobbies, manner of dress, popular movies and music, areas and cities of interest, holidays and the traditions practiced at each, geography and climate, and any other piece of Afghan culture that is mentioned in the novel.

DRAFTING

After you have completed your initial research, begin to think of the organization of your scrapbook. You may want to arrange things chronologically or by the topic you are discussing. For example, you may want to have a few pages in your scrapbook that outline important people and events in Afghanistan's history. On these pages, you may want to include powerful quotes from the novel along with photos and artwork you have found in your research. Each page should be colorful and creative and resemble a traditional scrapbook.

You may choose to put your pages together in a real scrapbook, use a notebook and construction paper to produce your final project, or make an "electronic scrapbook," creating a multimedia presentation. Regardless of the way in which you put it together, try to remember you want to make it attractive as well as informative. Include lists or bullet points to explain the photos and artwork you use, while remembering to tie in quotations from the novel. You may want to use a variety of picture shapes, multiple colors/prints, stickers, borders, and other fun methods typically found in a scrapbook. Your final scrapbook should have an attractive cover and include at least 15 pages covering a wide variety of cultural topics on Afghanistan.

Feel free to discuss what you find in the book with other students. You may share information, tips, and ideas, but each of you must complete your own unique scrapbook.

PROOFREADING

As you work on your scrapbook, ask others (family members, classmates, friends) to help you proofread and edit, so your final product will be accurate, interesting, and beautiful.

LESSON THREE

Objectives

1. To review main ideas, events, and vocabulary of Assignment 1
2. To create a visual display that will be used as an interactive reference resource during and after reading
3. To preview the vocabulary and study questions for Assignment 2
4. To read Assignment 2

Activity #1

Give students a few minutes to formulate answers for the study guide questions for Assignment 1, then discuss the answers to the questions in detail. Write the answers on the board or overhead transparency so students can have the correct answers for study purposes.

While students have their study guides out, preview the study questions for Assignment 2.

NOTE: It is a good practice in public speaking and leadership skills for individual students to take charge of leading the discussions of the study questions. Perhaps a different student could go to the front of the class and lead the discussion each day that the study questions are discussed in this unit. Of course, you should guide the discussion when appropriate and try to fill in any gaps students may leave. The study questions could really be handled in a number of different ways, including in small groups with group reports following. Occasionally you may want to use the multiple choice questions as quizzes to check students' reading comprehension. As a short review now and then, students could pair up for the first (or last, if you have time left at the end of a class period) few minutes of class to quiz each other from the study questions. Mix up methods of reviewing the materials and checking comprehension throughout the unit so students don't get bored just answering the questions the same way each day. Variety in methods will also help address the different learning styles of your students. From now on in this unit, the directions will simply say, "Discuss the answers to the study questions in detail as previously directed." You will choose the method of preparation and discussion each day based on what best suits you and your class.

Activity #2

Review the vocabulary answers from the reading. Make sure students write down the correct answers.

While students have their vocabulary worksheets out, do the worksheet for Assignment 2 together orally in class.

Activity #3

PRIOR TO CLASS:

Find a large map of the middle east and trace the outlines of Afghanistan and the surrounding countries onto a large piece of paper on your classroom bulletin board or wall.

During this class period, have students identify each of the countries and use different marker colors to label Afghanistan and the countries surrounding it. You may also want to have your students mark major cities in each country. After marking major locations, begin to add distinguishing marks to your map regarding the geography of the area. Students should identify mountains, deserts, and bodies of water on the map.

After you have the basic information about the area recorded, explain to students that this will be an interactive map that they will add to over the course of the book. Since you have just completed the first reading assignment, ask students to mark cities and landmarks mentioned in the first section of the novel.

<u>Activity #4</u>

Tell students that they should read Assignment 2 prior to the next class meeting. Give them the remainder of this class (if time remains) to work on this assignment.

LESSON FOUR

Objectives

1. To review main ideas, events, and vocabulary of Assignment 2
2. To have students research and read non-fiction related to the book to help connect the book to real life
3. To broaden students' knowledge about topics related to the book
4. To preview the vocabulary and study questions for Assignment 3
5. To read Assignment 3

Activity #1
Have students answer the study guide questions for reading Assignment 2 as previously directed. **While students have their study questions out, preview the questions for Assignment 3.**

Activity #2
Add events from the reading to the classroom map as previously described.

Activity #3
Take students to the library or media center. With students, brainstorm a list of non-fiction topics that could be related to *The Kite Runner*. A short list to get you started is included below.

-Islamic Religion
-The Taliban
-Events in Afghanistan's History
-Stories from people living in Afghanistan
-War on Terror
-America's relationship with the Middle East
-Hazara and Pashtun conflict
-Hazara Massacre
-Education in Afghanistan
-Zahir Shah
-Class structure in Afghanistan
-Women's rights in Afghanistan
-Technology and modernization in Afghanistan
-Kite Running/Kite Fighting Tournaments
-Surrounding Middle Eastern countries and their relationship with Afghanistan
-Stereotypes on Middle Eastern people
-Immigrants coming to America for a better life
-Customs and practices in Afghanistan
-Daily life in Afghanistan
-How Afghanistan has changed over the years
-How people in war torn countries are surviving in poverty

Activity #4
Distribute the Non-fiction Assignment Sheet to students. Explain that students should choose a non-fiction topic related to *The Kite Runner.* They should read a substantial article related to that topic and complete the Non-fiction Assignment Sheet for that article. Students may use magazines, newspapers, and the Internet as sources.

Activity #5
Bring the class back together and have each student tell what he/she read about.

Note: Compiling the Non-fiction Assignment Sheets into a booklet makes a nice follow-up activity and a handy reference for students.

Activity #6
Tell students that they should read Assignment 3 and do the related vocabulary worksheet prior to the next class period. Give them the remainder of this class (if time remains) to work on this assignment.

NON-FICTION AS IGNMENT SHEET
(To be completed after reading the required non-ˆiction article)

Name ________________________________ Date ____________________________

Title of Non-fiction Read ____

& ˙itten B(______________________ Publication Date ____________________

I. Factual ! mmˇ ˙(+& ˙″te a short summˇ ˙(of t˜e piece you read.

II. Vocabulary

1. With which vocabulary words in the piece did you encounter some deg˙ee of difficulty1

2. How did you resolve your lack of understanding with these words?

III. Interpretation: What was the main point the author wanted you to get from reading his work?

I- . Criticism

1. W″t˜ which points of the piece did you agree or find easy to accept1 & ˜(1

2. W″t˜ which points of the piece did you di,ˇ° ˙ee or find di˄˄″cult to bel″eve? & ˜(1

V. Personal Response: What do you t˜″nk about t˜″ s piece? <u>OR</u> How does t˜ ″, piece influence your ideas?

LESSON FIVE

Objectives

1. To write a short story like Amir's, with a lesson about life
2. To practice creative writing skills
3. To use character, setting, conflict, and other elements of fiction for the specific purpose of teaching a lesson about life
4. To appreciate the talents of the main character, Amir, as well as the author of *The Kite Runner*

Activity 1

In *The Kite Runner*, Amir decides to test his story telling abilities at a young age by writing a creative short story. He writes a short story that teaches readers a short moral lesson about greed and happiness. In this writing assignment, students will be asked to write their own creative short story that attempts to teach readers a lesson about life.

Re-read the passage in Chapter 7 beginning with "The streets glistened" (p. 60) through "...like snow collecting on a wall, one flake at a time" (p.64).

Point out the figurative language and imagery the author uses in these passages to bring them to life. Explain to students that figurative language is one tool the author has to help draw in the readers and develop the story. Ask students what other tools authors use to help draw readers into the story and develop characters, themes, and events throughout the story. [Answers should include things like connotation, dialogue, narration, etc.] Discuss examples of each.

Activity 2

Distribute Writing Assignment #1 and discuss the directions in detial. Give students ample time to complete the assignment and tell students when the assignment will be "due." Use the Writing Evaluation Form to give feedback to your students.

WRITING ASSIGNMENT #1 *The Kite Runner*

PROMPT

Amir sits down to write his first short story at a young age and receives compliments from both Rahim and Hassan about the story. In his short story, Amir teaches his readers a lesson about greed and happiness through the tale of a man who is able to turn his tears into pearls. Your assignment is to follow Amir's lead and create your own short story that teachers your readers an important lesson about life.

PREWRITING

Make a list of character flaws many people have, trying to focus on elements of character that can be changed. Items on your list should be simple character flaws like the need for power or control, greed, carelessness, rudeness, etc. Once you have created your list, select the character flaw you would like to write about and think of a creative way to warn people or prevent people from acting this way. As in Amir's story, the character with this flaw should find some benefit from his/her behavior until ultimately something happens to change his/her life and make them see the error of his/her ways.

DRAFTING

In your story you should provide readers with a setting, realistic characters and a basic plot structure. The beginning of your story should introduce the setting, characters, and conflict. The middle of your story should develop the conflict and allow the readers to see the real flaw of the character. The end of your story can have a positive or negative end for your character, as long as the readers are clear of the message you are trying to send and the character has seen the error of his or her ways.

PROMPT

When you finish the rough draft of your composition, ask a student who sits near you to read it. After reading your rough draft, he/she should tell you what he/she liked best about your work, which parts were difficult to understand, and ways in which your work could be improved. Reread your paper considering your critic's comments, and make the corrections you think are necessary. Ask your classmate what he/she thought of each of the characters/events you chose for your assignment.

PROOFREADING

Do a final proofreading of your paper double-checking your grammar, spelling, organization, and the clarity of your ideas.

WRITING EVALUATION FORM *The Kite Runner*

Name____________________________ Date __________

Writing Assignment # _______ Grade _________________

Circle One For Each Item:

Beginning:	excellent	good	fair	poor
Middle:	excellent	good	fair	poor
End:	excellent	good	fair	poor
Grammar:	excellent	good	fair	poor
Spelling:	excellent	good	fair	poor
Punctuation:	excellent	good	fair	poor
Legibility:	excellent	good	fair	poor
Creativity:	excellent	good	fair	poor
Moral/lesson:	excellent	good	fair	poor
__________:	excellent	good	fair	poor

Strengths:

Weaknesses:

Comments/Suggestions:

LESSON SIX

Objectives

1. To review main ideas, events, and vocabulary of Assignment 3
2. To bridge connections from the novel to the lives of students
3. To preview the vocabulary and study questions for Assignment 4
4. To read Assignment 4

Activity #1
Have students answer the study guide questions for reading Assignment 3 as previously directed. **While students have their study guides out, preview the questions for Assignment 4.**

Activity #2
Review the vocabulary answers from Assginment 3. Make sure students write down the correct answers. **Do the vocabulary worksheet for Assignment 4 orally together in class.**

Activity #3
Add events from the reading to the classroom map as previously described.

Activity #4
Students have just read about Amir's birthday party. Several of the study questions have dealt with the facts, but take a few minutes now to discuss these questions:

1. Was Amir's birthday a "success"?
2. What makes a birthday party successful?
3. What is the most important thing about a birthday party? Cake? Presents? Friends? Family? Feeling special, loved, appreciated?

Have students take out a piece of paper and write down characteristics of the birthday party of their dreams. Each student should make a list of the things his/her Most Wonderful Birthday Party Ever would have. Where would it be? Decorations? Guests? Activities? Presents? Tell students to think about WHY each of the elements of their Most Wonderful Birthday Parties Ever is important to them.

After students have had time to make their lists and think about them, ask for volunteers to share their best birthday dreams, then their best REAL birthdays--or the best real birthday parties they have attended.

Distribute the following Venn Diagram worksheet and tell students to fill it out comparing and contrasting their ideal, dream birthday party, Amir's party in the novel, and a real party of their own. In the lines provided at the bottom of the worksheet, have students write a concluding statement of their findings in comparing these three parties.

Activity #5
Tell students that they should read Assignment 4 prior to the next class meeting. Give them the remainder of this class (if time remains) to work on this assignment.

Comparing Three Things

item 1: ________________________ item 2: ________________________

item : ________________

Summary: ____

____

____

____

LESSON SEVEN

Objectives

1. To review main ideas, events, and vocabulary of Assignment 4
2. To practice writing to persuade
3. To preview the vocabulary and study questions for Assignment 5
4. To read Assignment 5

Activity #1
Have students answer the study guide questions for reading Assignment 4 as previously directed. **While students have their study questions out, preview the questions for Assignment 5.**

Activity #2
Add events from the reading to the classroom map as previously described.

Activity #3
Distribute Writing Assignment #2. Discuss the directions in detail, give students ample time to complete the assignment, and tell student when the assignment will be "due."

Activity #4
Tell students that they should read Assignment 5 and do the related vocabulary worksheet prior to the next class meeting. If students finish the writing assignment early, they may work on this assignment.

WRITING ASSIGNMENT #2 *The Kite Runner*

PROMPT
At the end of Chapter 7, Amir chooses not to defend Hassan when he is being raped. Your assignment is to rewrite the end of Chapter 7 starting with "It was the look of the lamb." You are there with Amir as his conscience. Try to convince him to go help his friend. Your attempt to convince him can either be successful or not, but if it is not successful, you should include what to say to him when he still chooses not to help Hassan.

PREWRITING
List reasons why Amir should help Hassan. Choose the most powerful reasons to use, and use the most effective way(s) of convincing Amir to help Hassan. Try to use at least two examples of figurative language in your scene re-write.

DRAFTING
You will probably have to write several drafts. Get the main gist of the scene ending down first, then re-write, substituting words and phrases as you work to find the most effective use of words and language to develop the scene and make your points.

PROMPT
When you finish the rough draft of your scene, ask a student who sits near you to read it. After reading your rough draft, he/she should tell you what he/she liked best about your work, which parts were difficult to understand, and ways in which your work could be improved. Reread your paper considering your critic's comments, and make the corrections you think are necessary.

PROOFREADING
Do a final proofreading of your paper double-checking your grammar, spelling, organization, and the clarity of your ideas.

LESSON EIGHT

Objectives

1. To bring ideas from the book into real life
2. To inform students about topics related to the novel
3. To practice listening skills

Activity

This day is set aside for a guest speaker. Invite one or more of the following people from your community to speak to your class:

-Someone who has relocated to America from Afghanistan
-News reporter or someone who has visited and researched Afghanistan
-College professor who specializes in Middle Eastern studies
-Someone from a local or national relief organization that works with people in Afghanistan
-Expert on the Islamic religion
-A kite builder or someone who is familiar with kite fighting
-Counselor or psychologist who can speak to the long term effects of guilt
-Military official or soldier who has been recently stationed in the Middle East
-Someone who helps immigrants get settled and acclimated to the United States
-Adoption agent who works with overseas adoptions

Divide your class time according to how many speakers you're able to acquire. Remember to allow time for students to ask questions. Let each speaker know how much time he/she will have for the presentation. Allow for time at the end of the class for students to make connections with what they have learned from the speakers with what they have read in *The Kite Runner*.

Follow Up: Be sure you and your students write thank you notes to each of your guests. At the very least, get a thank you card for each guest and have each of your students sign it (with any personal responses, if there is room).

LESSON NINE

Objectives

1. To review main ideas, events, and vocabulary of Assignment 5
2. To teach students about marriage customs in Afghanistan
3. To bridge connections with the novel to students' lives
4. To preview the vocabulary and study questions for Assignment 6
5. To read Assignment 6

Activity #1
Have students answer the study guide questions for reading Assignment 5 as previously directed. **While students have their study guides out, preview the questions for Assignment 6.**

Activity #2
Review the vocabulary answers from the reading. Make sure students write down the correct answers. **While students have their vocabulary work out, do the vocabulary worksheet for Assignment 6 orally together in class.**

Activity #3
Add events from the reading to the classroom map as previously described.

Activity #4
Show students clips from the popular TV shows *I Propose* and *A Wedding Story* (available as downloads from iTunes, and other places on the Internet). **Preveiw the clips entirely to be sure the content is appropriate for use in your classroom**.

[An alternate activity would be to have students discuss what they think would make the "perfect wedding."]

After the clips, talk to students about the engagement process in America and how couples typically meet and decide to marry. Next, brainstorm a list of wedding traditions in America as a class. Be sure to cover things like dress, music, location, decoration, ceremony, reception, and the honeymoon.

Visit an on-line web site to explore the engagement and wedding process in Afghanistan with your students. At the time of the printing of this LitPlan the following web site is available: (http://www.thepersianwedding.com/excerpt_en.html).

You may also want to have students reread the end of Chapter 12 and the beginning of Chapter 13 to see what specific customs Amir and Soraya follow.

After you have explored American and Afghan wedding traditions, give students the Venn diagram to fill out for the two cultures. Prompt students to find specific examples from their lives as well as the novel. On the back of the chart, have students write a short reflection on what they learned about Afghan weddings. Encourage them to find portions of the Afghan wedding that they think are good and explain why they like them.

Activity #5
Tell students that they should read Assignment 6 prior to the next class period. If time remains, give students the remainder of this class to work on this assignment.

Comparing Three Thingˇ

item 1: ____________________________ item 2: ____________________________

item : ____________________

Summary: ____

____

____

____

LESSON TEN

Objectives

1. To review main ideas, events, and vocabulary of Assignment 6
2. To preview the vocabulary and study questions for Assignment 7
3. To read Assignment 7
4. To evaluate students' oral reading
5. To discuss an assignment students will be working on that allows them to make a personal connection with the novel

Activity #1
Have students answer the study guide questions for Assignment 6 as previously directed. **Preview the questions for Assignment 7 while you have the study guides out.**

Activity #2
Do the vocabulary worksheet for Assignment 7 orally together in class.

Activity #3
Add events from the reading to the classroom map as previously described.

Activity #4
Have students read assignment 7 of *The Kite Runner* out loud in class. You probably know the best way to get readers with your class; pick students at random, ask for volunteers, or use whatever method works best for your group. If you have not yet completed an oral reading evaluation for your students, this would be a good opportunity to do so. A form is included with this unit for your convenience.

Activity #5
Amir and Hassan love the story about Rostam and Sohrab from the *Shahnamah.* Hassan is so affected by this tale that he names his son after his favorite character.

Use the Internet to find a copy of the story of Rostam and Sohrab (or a printed copy is available at www.tpet.com under *The Kite Runner* products).

Read this story to your class (or acquire copies of the story for your students to read).

When the reading is completed, discuss these questions:

1. Why would this story appeal to Amir and Hassan?

2. What connections can you find between this book and The Kite Runner? Are there any similarities or parallels?

3. Why would the author of *The Kite Runner* have chosen this particular book to be prominent in the story?

ORAL READING EVALUATION *The Kite Runner*

Name ____________________________ Class__________ Date __________________

SKILL	EXCELLENT	GOOD	AVERAGE	FAIR	POOR
Fluency	5	4	3	2	1
Clarity	5	4	3	2	1
Audibility	5	4	3	2	1
Pronunciation	5	4	3	2	1
____________	5	4	3	2	1
____________	5	4	3	2	1

Total ____________ Grade _______________

Comments:

LESSON ELEVEN

Objectives

1. To review main ideas, events, and vocabulary of Assignment 7
2. To help students understand how the Taliban control affected Afghanistan
3. To connect the lives of fictional characters in the novel to people in real life
4. To help students understand what life is like in Afghanistan
5. To preview the study questions and vocabulary for Assignment 8
6. To read Assignment 8

Activity #1
Have students answer the study guide questions for reading Assignment 7 as previously directed.

Activity #2
Review the vocabulary answers from the reading. Make sure students write down the correct answers.

Activity #3
Add events from the reading to the classroom map as previously described.

Activity #4
Ask students to site specific examples from the text regarding the changes Amir notices in his home country. Create a list of differences Amir sees after returning to his home and witnessing first hand the devastation from the Taliban rule. Ask students to reflect on what it must be like for Amir and others in Afghanistan to see a country they loved turned to ruin. You may also want to relate this feeling to victims of other disasters like hurricanes and tornados.

Activity #5
Rent or purchase the DVD titled *Afghan Stories* (available for sale at www.tpet.com under *The Kite Runner* title or from many other sources). This short documentary goes into Afghanistan and tells the story of several different people living in Afghanistan under the Taliban rule. This DVD allows students to meet real families and see the conditions they are living in. The DVD should help students to realize that the Afghan people are more than just terrorists by introducing them to normal families trying go get by.

[Afghan Stories is about an hour long, but you do not need to show the entire DVD; you could just show one or two stories from it to make the point.]

Show the video to your students and encourage them to take notes. After the film, give students 5-10 minutes to write a reflection on the documentary and how it has changed or shaped their perceptions. Once students have finished writing, allow students to share their views.

As an alternate activity, you could invite a few Afghan people from your community to come and tell students how the Taliban changed their lives.

Activity #6
Tell students that prior to the next class meeting they should preview the study questions, do the vocabulary worksheet, and complete the reading for Assignment 8.

LESSON TWELVE

Objectives

1. To review main ideas, events, and vocabulary of Assignment 8
2. To preview the study questions and vocabulary for Assignment 9
3. To read Assignment 9

Activity #1
Have students answer the study guide questions for reading Assignment 8 as previously directed. **Preview the questions for Assignment 9 while students have their study guides out.**

Activity #2
Review the vocabulary answers from Assignment 8. Make sure students write down the correct answers. **Do the vocabulary worksheet for Assignment 9 orally in class together.**

Activity #3
Add events from the reading to the classroom map as previously described.

Activity #4
Give students the remainder of the class to read Assignment 9. If you have not yet completed an oral reading evaluation for students this term, this is a good opportunity to do so. An evaluation form has been included in the unit for your convenience.

LESSON THIRTEEN

Objectives

1. To review the main events, ideas, and vocabulary from Assignment 9
2. To preview the study questions and vocabulary for Assignment 10
3. To read Assignment 10
4. To work on the scrapbook projects

Activity #1
Discuss the answers to the study questions for Assignment 9 as previously directed. **Preview the questions for Assignment 10 while students have their study guides out.**

Activity #2
Review the vocabulary answers from Assignment 9. Make sure students write down the correct answers. **Do the vocabulary worksheet for Assignment 10 orally in class together.**

Activity #3
Add events from Assignment 9 to the classroom map as previously directed.

Activity #4
Students should read Assignment 10 prior to the next class meeting. If you have not completed the oral reading evaluations (and wish to do so) now is a good time to finish them. Otherwise students may read silently or work on their scrapbook projects for the remainder of this class period.

LESSON FOURTEEN

Objectives

1. To review main ideas, events, and vocabulary from Assignment 10
2. To study indivdual characters and relationships in *The Kite Runner*
3. To work cooperatively in small groups

Activity #1

Discuss the study questions for Assignment 10, make sure all students have answers to the vocabulary worksheet, and update the classroom map as previously directed.

Activity #2

Divide your class into pairs or small groups, one for each of the following:

Amir
Hassan
Baba
Soraya
Sohrab
Assef
Ali
Rahim Kahn
General Taheri
Relationship between Amir and Baba
Relationship between Amir and Hassan
Relationship between Amir and Sohrab
Relationship between Amir and Soraya

Distribute the CHARACTER or CHARACTER RELATIONSHIP worksheets (whichever is appropriate) to the groups. Discuss the directions in detail and give students ample time to complete their work.

Come back together as a class to discuss the results of the groups' work via presentations and discussion.

CHARACTER WORKSHEET
The Kite Runner

Name of Character ____

Names of Group Members:

Adjectives for Physical Description of Character:

Adjectives for Description of Character's Personality:

What is the role of this character in the story?

Why is this character important in the story?

What are two important scenes in which the character appears?

Scene 1: Chapter ____ Page(s) _____
Description of the Scene:

Why this scene is important:

Scene 2: Chapter ___ Page(s) ___
Description of the Scene:

Why this scene is important:

Kite Runner Character Worksheet Page 2

What are two important quotes from this character? Justify why each is important.

Quote 1 (Chapter ___ Page ___):

Why this quote is important:

Quote 2 (Chapter ___ Page ___):

Why this quote is important:

What is this person's best character trait? Justify your answer.

What is this person's worst character trait? Justify your answer.

Would this person be considered a "good guy" or a "bad guy"? Why?

Additional notes or important relevant information about the character:

CHARACTER RELATIONSHIPS WORKSHEET
The Kite Runner

Names of Characters: Amir and ____________________________

Names of Group Members:

List three of the most important scenes involving these two characters (in which they both appear, interacting with one another) and explain why each scene is important.

Scene 1 [Chapter ___ Page(s) ___] Description:

Why this scene is important:

Scene 2 [Chapter ___ Page(s) ___] Description:

Why this scene is important:

Scene 3 [Chapter ___ Page(s) ___] Description:

Why this scene is important:

Kite Runner Character Relationship Worksheet Page 2

How does the relationship between these two characters change during the book?

What effect does the relationship with this person have on Amir?

What themes or ideas are presented to the reader through this relationship? Explain.

LESSON FIFTEEN

Objectives

1. To write to inform
2. To take the group character work and turn it into a written composition
3. To practice good writing skills
4. To evaluate students' writing skills and understanding of the group character work

Activtity

Distribute Writing Assignment #3 and discuss the directions in detail. Allow students ample time to complete the assignment, and tell students when the assignment will be due for grading.

WRITING ASSIGNMENT #3 *The Kite Runner*

PROMPT

In your group work and through class discussions you have done a lot of background work and thought a lot about a particular character or the relationship between two characters in *The Kite Runner*. Your assignment is to take the information you have about the character(s) and turn it into a written composition. Next year another class of students will read *The Kite Runner*. Write a composition in which you tell another student the most important things he/she should know about your character (or the relationship between your characters).

PREWRITING

Most of your prewriting work was done via the group work, worksheet, and class discussion. Now you need to look at all the information you have and decide how to organize and put it into a well-written format. How will you introduce your character or the characters' relationship? What main points do you want to make? Jot down these things and then make notes about how you want to organize and use them in your written work.

DRAFTING

You should have an introductory paragraph, several paragraphs in the body of your composition, and a concluding paragraph. Write, edit, and rewrite until you are satisfied that you have clearly stated all the main points you want to make.

PROMPT

When you have a final draft, have someone (whose advice you trust) read it and tell you what could be improved--areas that are perhaps unclear or not as well organized as they could be, grammatical or spelling errors that should be corrected, etc.

PROOFREADING

Consider the comments your independent reader made, make the corrections you feel are necessary, create a final copy and do a final proofreading.

LESSON SIXTEEN

Objectives

1. To review all of the vocabulary work done in this unit
2. To evaluate students' reaction to the unit
3. To provide feedback to the teacher regarding the unit

Activity #1

Choose one (or more) of the vocabulary review activities listed below and spend your class period as directed in the activity. Some of the materials for these review activities are located in the Vocabulary Resource Materials section in this LitPlan.

VOCABULARY REVIEW ACTIVITIES

1. Divide your class into two teams and have an old-fashioned spelling or definition bee.

2. Give each of your students (or students in groups of two, three or four) a *The Kite Runner* Vocabulary Word Search Puzzle. The person (group) to find all of the vocabulary words in the puzzle first wins.

3. Give students a *The Kite Runner* Vocabulary Word Search Puzzle without the word list. The person or group to find the most vocabulary words in the puzzle wins.

4. Use a *The Kite Runner* Vocabulary Crossword Puzzle. Put the puzzle onto a transparency on the overhead projector (so everyone can see it), and do the puzzle together as a class.

5. Give students a *The Kite Runner* Vocabulary Matching Worksheet to do.

6. Divide your class into two teams. Use *The Kite Runner* vocabulary words with their letters jumbled as a word list. Student 1 from Team A faces off against Student 1 from Team B. You write the first jumbled word on the board. The first student (1A or 1B) to unscramble the word wins the chance for his/her team to score points. If 1A wins the jumble, go to student 2A and give him/her a definition. He/she must give you the correct spelling of the vocabulary word which fits that definition. If he/she does, Team A scores a point, and you give student 3A a definition for which you expect a correctly spelled matching vocabulary word. Continue giving Team A definitions until some team member makes an incorrect response. An incorrect response sends the game back to the jumbled-word face off, this time with students 2A and 2B. Instead of repeating giving definitions to the first few students of each team, continue with the student after the one who gave the last incorrect response on the team. For example, if Team B wins the jumbled-word face-off, and student 5B gave the last incorrect answer for Team B, you would start this round of definition questions with student 6B, and so on. The team with the most points wins!

7. Have students write a story in which they correctly use as many vocabulary words as possible. Have students read their compositions orally! Post the most original compositions on your bulletin board!

Activity #2

Give students the Unit Reaction sheet. Give them a chance to answer the questions and give feedback about the unit. Read over the feedback and make any necessary adjustments to the unit before you begin to teach it the following year.

UNIT REACTION *The Kite Runner*

1. What were your overall impressions of *The Kite Runner*?

2. How likely are you to read one of Khaled Hosseini's other books?

3. How likely are you to read other fictional stories that take place in the Middle East?

4. What was your favorite assignment in the unit? Why?

5. What was your least favorite assignment in the unit? Why?

6. What was most helpful to you in this unit?

7. What assignment do you think should be changed? Why? How?

8. What was something that surprised you during this unit?

9. How did the research and information in the lessons affect you?

10. How has this unit affected your life (the decisions you make, how you view others, etc)?

Use the space below to write any other comments you have regarding this unit:

LESSONS SEVENTEEN AND EIGHTEEN

Objectives

1. To help students organize the events of the story and the feelings and experiences of each character
2. To discuss the novel on a deeper than direct-recall level
3. To prepare students for questions and topics covered on the test
4. To allow students to make personal connections with the text

Activity #1

Choose the questions from the Extra Discussion Questions/Writing Assignments which seem most appropriate for your students. A class discussion of these questions is most effective if students have been given the opportunity to formulate answers to the questions prior to the discussion. To this end, you may either have all the students formulate answers to all the questions, divide your class into groups and assign one or more questions to each group, or you could assign one question to each student in your class. The option you choose will make a difference in the amount of class time needed for this activity.

Note: The use of graphic organizers may be helpful to students in preparing their answers. Encourage them to use any diagrams or graphics that they feel are necessary.

EXTRA WRITING ASSIGNMENTS/DISCUSSION QUESTIONS *The Kite Runner*

Interpretive

1. Describe the author's writing style.
2. How does the point of view enhance the novel?
3. Under what genre does the story fall?
4. What are the main conflicts in the story? Describe each fully.
5. What is the setting, and what does it add to the story?
6. How does the author use events from history in the novel? What does this add to the story?

Critical

7. How does Amir foreshadow events to come later in the novel in the first two chapters?
8. What are the reader's first impressions of Hassan? How would you describe his personality and character?
9. What inferences can you make about Amir's father? What type of person is he? What type of father is he? Use details from the text to support your answer.
10. Though Hassan does not mention his mother, in what ways can the reader tell that Hassan misses her?
11. How do Ali's deformities contrast with his character?
12. What is the significance of what Amir reads about Hassan's people, the Hazaras, and his own people, the Pashtuns?
13. How are Amir and Hassan's first words important?
14. Amir's life is one of much more money and privilege than Hassan's. If he has such a better place in society and an easier life, why is he so jealous of his friend? In what ways does Amir reveal his jealously for the lowly Hazara?
15. Describe Amir's conflicting emotions with his father. Why is it that some days he worships him almost like a religion and on other days he wishes he were someone else's son?
16. Analyze how both Amir and his father are able to sting innocent people with their bitter words. Why do they do this? Is Amir more like his father than either of them thinks?
17. Describe the role Rahim plays in Amir's life as he is growing up. How does Amir's father feel about this role?
18. What type of relationship do Ali and Amir's father have? Would you expect this type of relationship given their history?
19. Compare and contrast Amir's typical school day with that of Hassan's.
20. Reread the excerpt from Amir and Hassan's favorite tale in the *Shahnamah,* located in Chapter 4. Why do you think both boys loved this tale so much? Explain each child's own hidden reasoning for enjoying this story.
21. Analyze Amir's first short story. Compare and contrast the ways Rahim's response and Hassan's response affected Amir and his confidence as a writer.
22. Why is Amir happy about the bombing and gunfire that took place in 1973?
23. What shift in the government took place in 1973? How did this change the lives of the characters in the story?

24. Assef idolizes Hitler and says, "If they had let Hitler finish what he had started, the world be a better place now." How does the vision of Hitler apply to Afghanistan? In what way does he hope Afghanistan will mimic what Hitler did?
25. Why does Amir struggle with calling Hassan a friend? In what ways is he like a friend? It what ways is he not? What does Amir's struggle over this "friendship" reveal?
26. Even when Hassan is being threatened and put down by Assef and his friends he uses the term "agha." What does this word mean? Why does Hassan use it even though these people clearly don't deserve his respect?
27. After Hassan has surgery to fix his cleft lip (that looks like a permanent smile) Amir says, "The swelling subsided, and the wound healed with time. Soon, it was just a pink jagged line running up from his lip. By the following winter, it was only a faint scar. Which was ironic. Because that was the winter that Hassan stopped smiling." What reasons does Hassan have to stop smiling?
28. Aside from being in better physical shape, why is Hassan better at chasing kites than Amir?
29. Why is it so hard for Amir to know that Hassan is completely loyal to him and means every word he says?
30. What clues tell the reader that Hassan is smarter and more insightful than Amir, even though he has never been educated?
31. What is the significance of Hassan's dream the night before the kite fighting tournament? Do you think he made this dream up? Why or why not?
32. Why does Amir think of his favorite story of Rostam and Sohrab after winning the kite fighting tournament?
33. As Amir is watching Hassan in the alley with Assef, he has a memory of a time when the two boys went to a fortune teller. What significance does the memory have? Why does this come to mind as he is watching Hassan endure painful ridicule and violence from the other boys? Amir also tells of a dream he had. What does this dream mean? Why does this come to mind at this time?
34. Amir says, 'I actually aspired to cowardice, because the alternative, the real reason I was running, was that Assef was right: Nothing is free in this world. Maybe Hassan was the price I had to pay, the lamb I had to slay, to win Baba.' How does Amir rationalize running away from his friend as he is being raped in the alley?
35. When Amir returns home as the kite fighting champion and with the last fallen kite he says, "It happened just the way I'd imagined." All his dreams about making his father proud had finally come true. However, Amir weeps. Was the outcome of making his father proud worth the means it took to get there? Was the moment tainted in any way after what it took to get there? Explain your answers using details from the text.
36. What clues does the author give to the reader to show that Rahim knows something more happened the night of the kite fighting tournament?
37. Amir says, "I understood the nature of my new curse: I was going to get away with it." What does he mean by this statement?
38. How does Amir's father react when Amir asks if he would ever get new servants? Why does he act this way?
39. Why can't Amir be friends with Hassan after the kite fighting tournament?
40. What is the significance of the scene where Amir throws pomegranates at Hassan?

41. Why does Amir toss all of his gifts in a pile in the corner of his room? Why doesn't he care about anything he received?
42. Why does Amir think getting rid of Hassan will lessen Hassan's suffering? Is he trying to lessen Hassan's suffering, or his own? Explain your answer using details from the text.
43. Why does Amir feel he is unworthy of the gift Hassan and Ali give him for his birthday?
44. Describe what happens when Amir's father confronts Hassan and Ali about stealing the watch and money. Be sure to include the realizations Amir has while watching the scene play out.
45. How does Amir know that Hassan saw him the night he was being raped?
46. What symbolism is present the day that Amir's father drives Hassan and Ali to the bus station?
47. Describe the state of Kabul when Amir and his father leave.
48. How is what happened to Kamal an example of irony?
49. How does Amir feel about the change of his father working so hard in Afghanistan to build a great life to his current life in California?
50. What does Amir's father mean when he says, "There are only three real men in this world, Amir...American the brash savior, Britain, and Israel. The rest of them they're like gossiping old women."?
51. Compare and contrast the different ways Amir and his father view America.
52. Amir's father refused food stamps and works hard to make a place for himself and his son in America. Compare and contrast the actions of his father with what you typically think of when you think of immigrants coming to America.
53. What does Amir's father say on the day of his graduation from high school that causes Amir to feel as if he can't breathe?
54. Amir and his father don't see eye to eye on Amir's college plans. Why is it so important for Amir to stand his ground and major in English like he plans?
55. Why does Amir compare the holiday of yelda to his relationship with Soraya?
56. Why does Amir have trouble finding doctors and getting treatment for his father?
57. When Amir finds out his father is dying he is overwhelmed with emotion. Amir is terrified about what he will do in life without his father. He dad responds by saying, "All those years, that's what I was trying to teach you, how to never have to ask that question." What does his father mean by this statement?
58. Describe the challenges Amir faces both physically and emotionally in dealing with his father's illness.
59. Why is Amir so understanding of Soraya's past? Why doesn't he care about the shameful things she has done?
60. Why does Amir envy Soraya for telling him her secret?
61. How does Amir's father feel about his son marrying Soraya? In what ways does the reader know his feelings?
62. Describe the Afghan marriage process and its customs from arranging the marriage to the end of the wedding night.
63. Compare and contrast the customs and traditions in an Afghan wedding with the customs and traditions in an American wedding.

64. Why does Amir cry when he sees Soraya reading his stories to his father as he is dying?
65. Amir says, 'Baba had wrestled bears his whole life. Losing his young wife. Raising a son by himself. Leaving his beloved homeland, his *watan.* Poverty. Indignity. In the end, a bear had come that he couldn't best. But even then he had lost on his own terms.' Why does Amir use a bear as a metaphor in this situation?
66. How does Amir feel after the death of his father? What realizations does he have? What scares him? What does he take with him?
67. As Amir's relationship with Soraya grows, he comes to know and understand more about her family. Compare and contrast Soraya's father with Amir's father.
68. Describe the relationship between Soraya's mother and father.
69. How does Amir's past continue to haunt him, even after all these years, in his married life?
70. Describe the condition of Afghanistan once the Russians finally leave.
71. How does Soraya feel about adoption? Why does she feel this way? How does her family feel about adoption? Why do they feel this way?
72. How does Amir know for certain that Rahim knows what happened after the kite fighting tournament and the events that followed?
73. How do relationships with parents and children change as they both grow older? Use both Amir and Soraya's relationships with their parents as the basis for your answer.
74. In what ways did the Taliban change Afghanistan?
75. Why is it surprising to hear Rahim tell Amir that when Ali almost died from polio when they were all kids, Amir's father, "walked around the house all day crying"?
76. How did Hassan react to hearing about Amir's father's death?
77. How does Amir react to the story of Hassan's death?
78. How does Amir handle Rahim's dying wish? How does he later handle the shocking news Rahim gives him?
79. What did Amir's father steal from him by lying about Hassan?
80. Amir says, "Baba and I were more alike than I'd ever known. We had both betrayed the people who would have given their lives for us. And with that came this realization: that Rahim Khan had summoned me here to atone not just for my sins but for Baba's too." What does he mean by this statement?
81. Why does Amir feel like a tourist in his own country? Why does Farid accuse him of being a tourist the entire time he lived there?
82. Why aren't other Afghan people welcoming to Amir?
83. Why does Amir get embarrassed when Afghans ask him about his writing?
84. What does Amir's dream of executing Hassan mean?
85. What emotional challenges does Amir face going back into Kabul?
86. Why are so many children without fathers? Why are so many children with mothers being placed in orphanages?
87. Amir realizes that his father never spoke of his mother, and that all of what he knows about his mother came from other people. Why did his father avoid speaking to him about his mother?
88. Who are the people behind the Taliban? How do they live?

89. Describe what Farid has been through in his childhood with the Russians and later in his adult life with the Taliban.
90. What happened to Assef after the Russians came in to Afghanistan?
91. As Amir is getting beaten to near death by Assef he says, "for the first time since the winter of 1975, I felt at peace." What does he mean by this?
92. Explain the irony of the situation when Sohrab hits Assef in the eye with a slingshot, saving Amir.
93. Why does the author use short, broken passages to tell the story of what is happening when Amir is first hospitalized?
94. How does the author continue to use the metaphor of the bear when Amir is hospitalized? What is the significance of this scene?
95. How is Amir's injury to his lip an example of irony?
96. What does Rahim say in his letter to Amir?
97. Why does Amir think he and his father were on better terms once they moved to America? How does their lifestyle relate to that of Hassan's lifestyle?
98. Sohrab flinches and pulls away every time Amir touches him. He is quiet most of the time and doesn't say much to Amir while he is recovering from his injuries. How does Amir build a relationship with Sohrab while they are in Pakistan?
99. Amir has a dream that Assef is standing in the doorway. Assef says to him, "We're the same, you and I...You nursed with him, but you're my twin." What does this dream mean?
100. How is Amir "able to be good again"?
101. Why does Sohrab run away to the mosque? What is he afraid of when it comes to God?
102. How does Sohrab react to finding out Amir is his uncle? How does Amir handle telling Sohrab such big news?
103. How does Soraya react to hearing the story Amir tells her about his childhood and what recently happened in Afghanistan?
104. How are Soraya's expectations about having Sohrab as a son different from reality?
105. Amir and Sohrab built a relationship in the time Amir was recovering from his injuries. What happens to damage this relationship?
106. What does Amir mean when he says, "I brought Hassan's son from Afghanistan to America, lifting him from the certainty of turmoil and dropping him in a turmoil of uncertainty."?
107. What epiphany does Amir have once back in America?
108. Why is Sohrab silent?
109. How does the author weave in the current tension between America and Afghanistan in his novel?
110. How does Amir's relationship with God grow and change throughout the novel?
111. What is the significance of the phrase, "for you a thousand times over"? How is it used throughout the novel?
112. How does the author leave the reader with a sense of hope at the end of the novel?
113. How does the author break American stereotypes of Afghanistan in this novel?
114. How does the author incorporate both guilt and atonement in the novel? What was he trying to say about both of these feelings?

Critical/Personal Response

115. How would you describe Amir's early years in Kabul? Give ways Amir's childhood was both similar and different from your own.

116. Amir is very surprised to read about the Pashtuns, his people, and the Hazaras, Hassan's people. He is shocked to see that his school textbook leaves out this important time in Afghanistan's history. Why do you think this is left out of the textbooks? Do you think important information is ever left out of your textbooks? Give an example of something barely mentioned in your course books that should be studied in more detail.

117. Why does Amir feel like his father always hated him a little? Do you think his rationalization of this feeling is true? How would you feel towards your son if you were in Baba's situation?

118. Amir's father pushes him to play soccer and enjoy sports, just as he does. Do you think his father is helping or hurting their relationship by trying to teach him about things he loves? Have your parents ever tried to push you to enjoy and participate in the same things they love? How did it feel? How did it affect your relationship if you didn't have the same interests?

119. Why doesn't Amir think of Hassan as a friend? Would you think of the two as friends? Explain why or why not.

120. Amir thinks nothing of Hassan's illiteracy, and is not surprised that all Hazaras are uneducated, since they are all of a low place in society and are typically servants. Do you think people in our society are denied an equal education based on their race or level of income? Explain your answer.

121. Amir says that none of them had ever heard gunfire in the streets. Does that surprise you? Why or why not? How do people in Afghanistan now live?

122. Amir says, "Baba and I lived in the same house, but in different spheres of existence. Kites were the one paper-thin slice of intersection between those spheres." How do kites help mend Amir's relationship with his father? Have you ever had an interest you shared with someone in your family that allowed you to bond in a special way? Give details from the novel and your life to support your answer.

123. Amir is constantly struggling for love and attention from his father, blindly loving him despite the pain he feels from disappointing him. How is this relationship similar to the one between Amir and Hassan? How can Amir feel so much pain and treat someone else the same way?

124. What does it mean to own something American in Afghanistan? What does it mean for Americans to own something foreign, especially from Europe? Why do you think people tend to feel this way?

125. What could Hassan have done to avoid being raped by Assef? Why doesn't he take the easy way out and just give him what he wanted to avoid this type of pain? What does this reveal about his character?

126. Rahim tells Amir about how he almost married a Hazara. He concludes the story with, "In the end, the world always wins." Do you think Rahim made the right choice? Do you agree that the world always wins? Explain your answer.

127. Hassan knows that Amir watched as he was raped and did nothing to help him. Yet over and over, Hassan proves his love and loyalty to Amir. Why do you think this is? Does he deserve this type of loyalty, why or why not? Have you ever witnessed this type of loyalty in your lifetime?

128. What does Amir's father think of the United States' decision to boycott the Olympic Games in Moscow? Do you agree or disagree with his view? Why?

129. Amir admits that there is an Afghan double standard for men and women. Though he and Soraya are both engaging in unsupervised conversation, she will be the one gossiped about around the community, not him. Do you think this is fair? Explain your answer. Do you think there is a double standard in America with men and women? Use observations from your life to support your answer.

130. When Amir talks about his father he says, "I think the only thing he loved as much as his late wife was Afghanistan." Compare and contrast his father's love for his country with the love Americans have for their country.

131. Amir says, "It hit me again, the enormity of what I had done that winter and following summer." How do you think it felt for Amir to return to Pakistan to see Rahim? How do you think it felt for him to discover that Hassan was still a loyal and loving friend, even after what happened?

132. Amir finds out that his whole life has been built around a lie. How did this news affect him? Do you think this explained anything for him? How would you have handled this news?

133. As Amir enters Kabul for the first time he says, 'A sadness came over me. Returning to Kabul was like running into an old, forgotten friend and seeing that life hadn't been good to him, that he'd become homeless and destitute.' How hard is this trip for Amir? How would you handle this situation if you were him? How would you react to the devastation you are witnessing?

134. The director of the orphanage says, "I haven't been paid in over six months. I'm broke because I've spent my life's savings on this orphanage. Everything I ever owned or inherited I sold to run this godforsaken place. You think I don't have family in Pakistan and Iran? I could have run like everyone else. But I didn't. I stayed. I stayed because of them...If I deny him one child, he takes ten. So I let him take one and leave the judging to Allah. I swallow my pride and take his goddamn filthy...dirty money. Then I go to the bazaar and buy food for the children." Do you agree with this rationalization? How do you think the director feels knowing what he does? Do you think he is still helping people?

135. The Taliban claims to be doing God's work through all their violent actions. Do you think their actions can be justified by religion? Do others of this same religion agree with the Taliban's take on God? Should anyone ever have the right to make these types of decisions based on their religion?

136. How does Sohrab first react around Amir? Would you expect this type of behavior from him? Why or why not?

137. Rahim tells Amir in his letter to finally forgive himself. What does Amir have to forgive himself for? Do you think forgiveness will be easy after all that has happened in this trip to Afghanistan, or will he always be haunted by his decision as a child? Explain your answer.

138. How would you describe Amir's parenting skills? What does he do well? What does he need to improve on?

Personal Response

139. Amir says he became who he is today at the age of twelve. Can you think of a time or an event in your life that significantly changed you in a way that affected who you are today? Explain your answer.

140. Amir's father tells him, 'There is only one sin, only one. And that is theft. Every other sin is a variation of theft.' Do you agree or disagree with his view? Is every other type of sin essentially robbing someone else of something? What do you view as the worst sin? Why?

141. Amir says, "That was how I escaped my father's aloofness, in my dead mother's books." How do you escape your problems in life? Have books ever been a way for you to escape to another world? Explain why or why not.

142. Assef is a bully, and yet at the same time, is able to sweet talk adults and gain the admiration of Amir's father. Do you know anyone in your life that is like Assef? Do you know anyone who is able to turn on the charm in one setting, and be completely different in another? Explain how this makes you feel to see both sides of someone's character and know the real truth.

143. What are your first impressions of the kite fighting tournament? Were you surprised by any of the practices or customs? Would you participate in this tournament? Why or why not? Can you think of any tournaments Americans have that others might find unusual?

144. "I opened my mouth, almost said something. Almost. The rest of my life might have turned out differently if I had. But I didn't. I just watched." Amir's life changed because he was too afraid to say something and just stood by to watch. Has there ever been a time in your life where you neglected to say or do the right thing that then haunted you later? Explain how this made you feel.

145. Amir says, "I finally had what I'd wanted all those years. Except now that I had it, I felt as empty as this unkempt pool I was dangling my legs into." Have you ever wanted something so bad, but when you finally got it you were disappointed or unsatisfied? Why didn't you feel like you imagined? How were you able to move past this disappointment?

146. Amir's father has a very difficult time adjusting to life in America. How would you feel if you were forced to leave everything you owned in another country and flee to somewhere new? What difficulties would you have? How would you deal with these challenges?

147. Amir says, "I cringed a little at the position of power I'd been granted, and all because I had won at the genetic lottery that had determined my sex." Do you think men in America hold a certain power due to their gender? Explain why or why not.

148. Amir's father refused any medical treatment for his cancer. The doctors tell him "it wouldn't change the outcome, just prolong it." What would you do in this situation? Do you agree or disagree with his decision to refuse treatment? Why do you feel this way?

149. Amir and Soraya marry without having known each other for very long, and without getting to date. What do you think of the way their marriage is arranged? Do you think this custom is better or worse than the custom of marrying for love in America? Will one work better than the other? Explain your answer.

150. Rahim says, "I see America has infused you with the optimism that has made her so great." Do you think the optimism people in America have about life is a good or bad quality? Explain your answer.

151. Hassan takes his mother in after all those years of never once hearing from her. He knows she willingly abandoned him as a child, and yet he cares for her and loves her as if nothing had happened. Would you be able to do the same thing in his situation? Why or why not?

152. Amir's mother once said, "I'm so profoundly happy...Happiness like this is frightening...They only let you be this happy if they're preparing to take something from you." Do you agree or disagree with her statement? Why or why not?

153. How did you feel reading about Amir's trip back into Kabul? What scenes were hard for you to handle while reading? What were you feeling? Does reading about the rape of children and extreme poverty make you want to do something to help other parts of the world?

154. How has reading this novel changed or shaped your perceptions about Afghanistan?

Quotes Worksheet *The Kite Runner*

1. "I became what I am today at the age of twelve, on a frigid overcast day in the winter of 1975."

2. "It's wrong what they say about the past, I've learned, about how you can bury it. Because the past claws its way out."

3. "Then he would remind us that there was a brotherhood between people who had fed from the same breast, a kinship that not even time could break."

4. "Children aren't coloring books. You don't get to fill them with your favorite colors."

5. "A boy who won't stand up for himself becomes a man who can't stand up to anything."

6. "Because history isn't easy to overcome. Neither is religion. In the end, I was a Pashtun and he was a Hazara, I was Sunni and he was Shi'a, and nothing was ever going to change that. Nothing."

7. "That Hassan would grow up illiterate like Ali and most Hazaras had been decided the minute he had been born...what use did a servant have for the written word?"

8. "The generation of Afghan children whose ears would know nothing but the sounds of bombs and gunfire was not yet born."

9. Afghanistan is the land of the Pashtuns. It always has been, always will be. We are the true Afghans, the pure Afghans, not this Flat-Nose here. His people pollute our homeland, our *watan.* They dirty our blood...I'll ask the president to do what the king didn't have the *quwat* to do. To rid Afghanistan of all the dirty, *kasseef* Hazaras.

10. "I was going to win, and I was going to run that last kite. Then I'd bring it home and show it to Baba. Show him once and for all that his son was worthy. Then maybe my life as a ghost in this house would finally be over...And maybe, just maybe, I would finally be pardoned for killing my mother."

11. "'For you a thousand times over!' he said. Then he smiled his Hassan smile and disappeared around the corner. The next time I saw him smile unabashedly like that was twenty-six years later, in a faded Polaroid photograph."

12. "I opened my mouth, almost said something. Almost. The rest of my life might have turned out differently if I had. But I didn't. I just watched."

13. "Then I understood: This was Hassan's final sacrifice for me. If he'd said no, Baba would have believed him because we all knew Hassan never lied. And if Baba believed him, then I'd be the accused; I would have to explain and I would be revealed for what I really was...He knew I had betrayed him and yet he was rescuing me once again, maybe for the last time."

14. "But theft was the one unforgivable sin, the common denominator of all sins...And if Baba could forgive that, then why couldn't he forgive me for not being the son he'd always wanted?"

15. "Strangely, I was glad someone knew me for who I really was; I was tired of pretending."

16. Russian solider: "There is no shame in war." Amir's father: "Tell him he's wrong. War doesn't negate decency. It demands it, even more than in times of peace."

17. "Israel was an island of 'real men' in a sea of Arabs too busy getting fat off their oil to care for their own."

18. "But I would stand my ground, I decided. I didn't want to sacrifice for Baba anymore. The last time I had done that, I had damned myself."

19. "How could I, of all people, chastise someone for their past?"

20. "There was so much goodness in my life. So much happiness. I wondered whether I deserved any of it."

21. "Come. There is a way to be good again,..."

22. "The conversation inevitably turned to the Taliban. 'Is it as bad as I head?' I said. 'Nay, it's worse. Much worse, he said. 'They don't let you be human.'"

23. "The infighting between the factions was fierce and no one knew if they would live to see the end of the day. Our ears became accustomed to the whistle of falling shells, to the rumble of gunfire, our eyes familiar with the sight of men digging bodies out of piles of rubble. Kabul in those days, Amir jan, was as close as you could get to that proverbial hell on earth."

24. "Amir jan, I summoned you here because I wanted to see you before I die, but that is not all...I want you to go to Kabul. I want you to bring Sohrab here."

25. "I looked at the round face in the Polaroid again, the way the sun fell on it. My brother's face. Hassan had loved me once, loved me in a way that no one ever had or ever would again. He was gone now, but a little part of him lived on. It was in Kabul. Waiting."

26. "Once, over those mountains, I had made a choice. And now, a quarter of a century later, that choice had landed me right back on this soil."

27. "Door to door we went, calling for the men and the boys. We'd shoot them right there in front of their families. Let them see. Let them remember who they were, where they belonged...Sometimes, we broke down their doors and went inside their homes. And...I'd...I'd sweep the barrel of my machine gun around the room, and fire and fire until the smoke blinded me...You don't know the meaning of the world 'liberating' until you've done that, stood in a roomful of targets, let the bullets fly, free of guilt and remorse, knowing you are virtuous, good, and decent. Knowing you're doing God's work."

28. "What mission is that...Stoning adulterers? Raping children? Flogging women for wearing high heels? Massacring Hazaras? All in the name of Islam?"

29. "I hadn't been happy and I hadn't felt better, not at all. But I did now. My body was broken--just how badly I wouldn't find out until later--but I felt healed. Healed at last."

30. "A man who has no conscience, no goodness, does not suffer. I hope your suffering comes to an end with this journey to Afghanistan."

31. "And that, I believe, is what true redemption is, Amir jan, when guilt leads to good."

32. "There are a lot of children in Afghanistan, but little childhood."

33. "It was only a smile, nothing more. It didn't make everything all right. It didn't make anything all right. Only a smile. A tiny thing. A leaf in the woods, shaking in the wake of a startled bird's flight. But I'll take it. With open arms. Because when spring comes, it melts the snow one flake at a time, and maybe I just witnessed the first flake melting."

LESSON NINETEEN

Objectives

1. To review the main ideas and events in *The Kite Runner*
2. To allow students to practice writing a letter
3. To allow students to show the author their appreciation for the book

Activity #1
Choose one of the review games/activities suggested in this unit and spend your class time as directed there.

REVIEW GAMES/ACTIVITIES *The Kite Runner*

1. Ask the class to make up a unit test for *The Kite Runner.* The test should have 4 sections: matching, true/false, short answer, and essay. Students may use 1/2 period to make the test and then swap papers and use the other 1/2 class period to take a test a classmate has devised. (open book) You may want to use the unit test included in this packet or take questions from the students' unit tests to formulate your own test.

2. Take 1/2 period for students to make up true and false questions (including the answers). Collect the papers and divide the class into two teams. Draw a big tic-tac-toe board on the chalk board. Make one team X and one team O. Ask questions to each side, giving each student one turn. If the question is answered correctly, that students' team's letter (X or O) is placed in the box. If the answer is incorrect, no letter is placed in the box. The object is to get three in a row like tic-tac-toe. You may want to keep track of the number of games won for each team.

3. Take 1/2 period for students to make up questions (true/false and short answer). Collect the questions. Divide the class into two teams. You'll alternate asking questions to individual members of teams A & B (like in a spelling bee). The question keeps going from A to B until it is correctly answered, then a new question is asked. A correct answer does not allow the team to get another question. Correct answers are +2 points; incorrect answers are -1 point.

4. Have students pair up and quiz each other from their study guides and class notes.

5. Give students a *The Kite Runner* crossword puzzle to complete.

6. Play What's My Line?. This is similar to the old television show. Students assume the roles of different characters from the novel. One student gives clues to the class, or to a panel of contestants. The contestants try to guess the identity of the guest. Students may enjoy assisting you in creating rules and procedures for the game.

7. Divide your class into two teams. Use *The Kite Runner* crossword words with their letters jumbled as a word list. Student 1 from Team A faces off against Student 1 from Team B. You write the first jumbled word on the board. The first student (1A or 1B) to unscramble the word wins the chance for his/her team to score points. If 1A wins the jumble, go to student 2A and give him/her a clue. He/she must give you the correct word which matches that clue. If he/she does, Team A scores a point, and you give student 3A a clue for which you expect another correct response. Continue giving Team A clues until some team member makes an incorrect response. An incorrect response sends the game back to the jumbled-word face off, this time with students 2A and 2B. Instead of repeating giving clues to the first few students of each team, continue with the student after the one who gave the last incorrect response on the team. For example, if Team B wins the jumbled-word face-off, and student 5B gave the last incorrect answer for Team B, you would start this round of clue questions with student 6B, and so on. The team with the most points

wins!

8. Play Jeopardy. Divide the class into two groups. Assign each group a category or book from the novel and have them devise answers for that category. Play the game according to the television show procedures.

9. Play Drawing in the Details. This is similar to Pictionary. Divide students into teams. A student from one team draws a scene from the novel. (You may want to specify the Book or section.) Drawings should be kept simple, to keep the pace lively. Students in the opposing team locate the scene in their books and read it aloud. If they are incorrect, the illustrator's team has a chance to guess. Involve students in setting up a scoring system and any other necessary rules.

10. Take students to a school soccer field. Divide students into two teams. Have student A from team 1 answer a question. If he/she gets it correct, he/she can take a penalty kick for an extra point. Next, allow student B from team 2 to answer a question. If the answer is correct he/she can take a penalty kick for a bonus point. Continue to ask questions awarding one point for a correct answer and one bonus point for a goal. Point out that part of the reason for the review is based on Amir's experience at the soccer game as well as Baba's love for the sport.

Activity #2
Give students the Letter to the Author Assignment Sheet. If needed, review how to write a formal letter with your students. Give them the remainder of the class time to complete the letter. Once you have proofread all the letters and students have had the chance to correct any mistakes, mail the letters to Khaled Hosseini:

Khaled Hosseini
Penguin Group (USA) Inc
c/o Riverhead Books Publicity
375 Hudson Street
New York, NY 100143

Note: This assignment may be used as an extra credit opportunity. You may offer extra credit for simply writing the letter, or offer extra credit for those who type their letter.

Letter to the Author

Often times, books are written to make people think about serious issues. Think about the point the author was trying to make in writing this book. Then, compose a letter to the author expressing how this book has affected your life.

Topics to include in your letter:

- What you liked about the book
- How you could relate to this book
- How realistic the book was
- What you learned from the book
- What issues the book made you think about
- How you felt when reading the book
- How you have changed since reading the book
- Anything else you think the author should know

Necessary Elements:

- Your letter must by typed
- You should begin your letter by saying Dear Ms. ____________________,
- You should have an introductory paragraph where you introduce yourself
- You should have body paragraphs
- You should have a friendly conclusion to the letter
- Underneath your signature you should include your home address and email address in case the author wishes to write you back

Remember to proofread this letter and turn it in to me free of errors. I will grade your letter, allow you to make any changes that are needed, and then I will mail your letters to the author of your book. Most authors enjoy receiving letters from readers and like to see how their hard work has affected others. Some authors even respond to letters from their readers, so don't be surprised if you get a reply.

LESSON TWENTY

Objectives
To test the students' understanding of the main ideas and themes in *The Kite Runner*

Activity #1
Distribute the unit tests. Go over the instructions in detail and allow the students the entire class period to complete the exam.

NOTE: There are 5 different unit tests included in the LitPlan Teacher Pack. Two are short answer, two are multiple choice. There is one advanced short answer test. The answers to the advanced short answer test will be based on the discussions you have had during class and should be graded accordingly. You should choose the tests and/or test parts which best suit your needs. Matching and short answer tests have answer keys. For essay type questions, grade according to your own criteria based on class discussions and the level of your students. Also, you will need to choose vocabulary words to read orally for the vocabulary section of the short answer tests.

Activity #2
Collect all test papers and assigned books prior to the end of the class period.

LESSON TWENTY-ONE (Optional)

Objectives

1. To provide students an opportunity to create a kite to fight with others as done in the novel
2. To expose students to music and hobbies of the Afghanistan culture

Activity #1

This day is set aside to expose your students to the culture of Afghanistan. Since kite fighting plays such an important role in both the beginning and end of the novel, students should have the opportunity to create a kite and experience kite fighting for the first time. Instructions for building a kite can be found online along with simple blueprints for students to trace. You can make a kite out of something as simple as a piece of paper, string, and pipe cleaners, or you can work with your class to create more advanced, attractive kites. It might be advisable to have students bring materials from home to create their own kites if you choose to do something more elaborate. Use this day to create the kites and allow them to dry (if students choose to decorate them) and fly the kites at the end of lesson 21.

On this day it is also advised that you expose your students to other positive aspects of the Afghan culture. Download contemporary Afghan music, and also the music of Ahmad Zahir, who is mentioned in the novel several times. You may also want to have students bring in traditional Afghan food, or money to cater Afghan food from a local restaurant. Suggestions include the kabobs and naan Amir mentions several times in the novel.

UNIT TESTS

The Kite Runner SHORT ANSWER UNIT TEST 1

I. MATCHING/IDENTIFY

____ 1.	RAHIM	A.	Hassan is born with a deformity on his __________.
____ 2.	FACE	B.	Sohrab takes a long one of these each night before he goes to bed.
____ 3.	LIP	C.	Ali's ______ and leg are both crippled/paralyzed.
____ 4.	THEFT	D.	Amir works to raise money for a _________ in Afghanistan.
____ 5.	KNUCKLES	E.	The man in the Taliban with the dark sunglasses turns out to be ___________.
____ 6.	HITLER	F.	Best friend and business partner to Amir's father
____ 7.	SLINGSHOT	G.	Ali is killed by stepping on one of these.
____ 8.	LAST	H.	Weapon used by both Hassan and Sohrab to save Amir
____ 9.	GLASS	I.	Amir's chosen career
____ 10.	KARIM	J.	Place where Hassan was shot and killed
____ 11.	BASEMENT	K.	This is on the spool of the kite to help with kite fighting.
____ 12.	TEACHER	L.	He smuggles people out of Afghanistan to safety in Pakistan.
____ 13.	AUTHOR	M.	Person Assef idolizes
____ 14.	PREGNANT	N.	Soraya's ________ is able to help get Sohrab into America.
____ 15.	MINE	O.	Soraya's chosen profession
____ 16.	STREET	P.	Amir's father believes ____ is the root of all other sins.
____ 17.	ASSEF	Q.	Amir, his father, and several other people wait here while the truck is repaired to go to Pakistan.
____ 18.	BATH	R.	Despite how hard she tried, Soraya could not get ____________.
____ 19.	UNCLE	S.	The __________ kite to fall is the most coveted by kite runners.
____ 20.	HOSPITAL	T.	Assef is known for carrying around brass ____________.

II. SHORT ANSWER

1. How did Amir's family come to know Ali?

2. What does it mean to "run" a kite?

3. Why does Amir want to win the kite tournament so badly?

4. What happens to Hassan after he has caught the last fallen kite from the tournament?

5. Describe Amir's relationship with his father after winning the tournament.

6. How does Amir's father react when Ali quits?

7. How do Amir and his father travel on the second leg of their trip to safety?

8. How did the people of Afghanistan react when the Taliban took control of the country?

9. What shocking news does Rahim tell Amir?

10. What does the director of the orphanage say happened to Sohrab?

11. What happens at half time during the soccer game?

12. Why does Amir start laughing when he is in so much pain?

13. Describe how Amir is finally able to leave the room and get away to safety with Sohrab.

14. What is the significance of Amir's injury to his lip?

15. What happens at this celebration that makes Sohrab smile?

III. ESSAY

1. What is the significance of the phrase, "for you a thousand times over"? How is it used throughout the novel?

2. How does the author leave the reader with a sense of hope at the end of the novel?

IV. Vocabulary

A. Write the vocabulary words you are given. After writing them down, go back and write in their definitions.

Word	Definition
1	
2	
3	
4	
5	
6	
7	
8	
9	
10	

The Kite Runner SHORT ANSWER UNIT TEST 1 Answer Key

I. MATCHING/IDENTIFY

F	1. RAHIM	A. Hassan is born with a deformity on his __________.
C	2. FACE	B. Sohrab takes a long one of these each night before he goes to bed.
A	3. LIP	C. Ali's ______ and leg are both crippled/paralyzed.
P	4. THEFT	D. Amir works to raise money for a _________ in Afghanistan.
T	5. KNUCKLES	E. The man in the Taliban with the dark sunglasses turns out to be ___________.
M	6. HITLER	F. Best friend and business partner to Amir's father
H	7. SLINGSHOT	G. Ali is killed by stepping on one of these.
S	8. LAST	H. Weapon used by both Hassan and Sohrab to save Amir
K	9. GLASS	I. Amir's chosen career
L	10. KARIM	J. Place where Hassan was shot and killed
Q	11. BASEMENT	K. This is on the spool of the kite to help with kite fighting.
O	12. TEACHER	L. He smuggles people out of Afghanistan to safety in Pakistan.
I	13. AUTHOR	M. Person Assef idolizes
R	14. PREGNANT	N. Soraya's ________ is able to help get Sohrab into America.
G	15. MINE	O. Soraya's chosen profession
J	16. STREET	P. Amir's father believes ____ is the root of all other sins.
E	17. ASSEF	Q. Amir, his father, and several other people wait here while the truck is repaired to go to Pakistan.
B	18. BATH	R. Despite how hard she tried, Soraya could not get ____________.
N	19. UNCLE	S. The __________ kite to fall is the most coveted by kite runners.
D	20. HOSPITAL	T. Assef is known for carrying around brass _____________.

II. SHORT ANSWER

1. How did Amir's family come to know Ali?
Ali's parents were hit by impaired drivers. The drivers were brought before Amir's grandfather, the judge, along with the orphaned son, Ali. After the trial, Amir's grandfather adopted Ali and he was raised alongside Amir's father.
2. What does it mean to "run" a kite?
A kite runner is someone who runs all around the city trying to catch a falling kite before it lands.
3. Why does Amir want to win the kite tournament so badly?
Amir realizes this is a way to gain his father's love and affection and to finally make him proud.
4. What happens to Hassan after he has caught the last fallen kite from the tournament?
He is raped by Assef.
5. Describe Amir's relationship with his father after winning the tournament.
He and his father spend a lot of time together. They see movies together, visit the zoo, and go on trips. His father agrees to everything Amir asks, and the two talk more than ever.
6. How does Amir's father react when Ali quits?
He begs them not to leave and tells them they are forgiven. He cries, which is something Amir has never seen his father do.
7. How do Amir and his father travel on the second leg of their trip to safety?
They are put into an empty fuel tank with several others. There is absolutely no light, the air they breathe is full of gasoline fumes, and they cannot move or get out for quite some time.
8. How did the people of Afghanistan react when the Taliban took control of the country?
They were happy, they celebrated and danced in the streets because they thought it was an end to the war and their country would once again know peace.
9. What shocking news does Rahim tell Amir?
Rahim explains that Ali was sterile and could not have children. He then alludes to the fact that Amir's father was also Hassan's father. He had gotten Hassan's mother pregnant so Ali could have a child, and they kept it a secret all this time. Amir and Hassan were actually half brothers.
10. What does the director of the orphanage say happened to Sohrab?
Once a month a Taliban official comes to the orphanage and takes a child for his pleasure. A month ago, this man took Sohrab.
11. What happens at half time during the soccer game?
The Taliban bring out a man and a woman and places them both in a chest-deep hole behind the goalpost. A leading member of the Taliban comes out and stones them to death as the crowd watches.
12. Why does Amir start laughing when he is in so much pain?
He realizes that for the first time since the winter of 1975 he is at peace, even though he is getting severely beaten.
13. Describe how Amir is finally able to leave the room and get away to safety with Sohrab.
Sohrab picks up a brass ball off the bottom of the table and puts it in his slingshot. He asks Assef to stop, and when he doesn't he shoots him in the eye. Assef loses his eye and is in great pain.
14. What is the significance of Amir's injury to his lip?
Hassan was harelipped and had a scar in the same place above his mouth. Now, Amir has the same exact scar that Hassan had.

15. What happens at this celebration that makes Sohrab smile?
    He flies a kite with Amir. The two fight another kite and win the tournament.

IV. Vocabulary

A. Write the vocabulary words you are given. After writing them down, go back and write in their definitions.

Word	Definition
1	
2	
3	
4	
5	
6	
7	
8	
9	
10	

Select the vocabulary words for Short Answer Test 1

The Kite Runner SHORT ANSWER UNIT TEST 2

I. MATCHING/IDENTIFY

____ 1.	RAHIM	A.	He smuggles people out of Afghanistan to safety in Pakistan.
____ 2.	FACE	B.	Ali is killed by stepping on one of these.
____ 3.	LIP	C.	Hassan is born with a deformity on his __________.
____ 4.	THEFT	D.	Amir, his father, and several other people wait here while the truck is repaired to go to Pakistan.
____ 5.	KNUCKLES	E.	Weapon used by both Hassan and Sohrab to save Amir
____ 6.	HITLER	F.	Best friend and business partner to Amir's father
____ 7.	SLINGSHOT	G.	Soraya's ________ is able to help get Sohrab into America.
____ 8.	LAST	H.	Person Assef idolizes
____ 9.	GLASS	I.	Amir's father believes ____ is the root of all other sins.
____ 10.	KARIM	J.	Soraya's chosen profession
____ 11.	BASEMENT	K.	Assef is known for carrying around brass _____________.
____ 12.	TEACHER	L.	The __________ kite to fall is the most coveted by kite runners.
____ 13.	AUTHOR	M.	Place where Hassan was shot and killed
____ 14.	PREGNANT	N.	Amir works to raise money for a _________ in Afghanistan.
____ 15.	MINE	O.	Sohrab takes a long one of these each night before he goes to bed.
____ 16.	STREET	P.	This is on the spool of the kite to help with kite fighting.
____ 17.	ASSEF	Q.	Amir's chosen career
____ 18.	BATH	R.	Despite how hard she tried, Soraya could not get ____________.
____ 19.	UNCLE	S.	Ali's ______ and leg are both crippled/paralyzed.
____ 20.	HOSPITAL	T.	The man in the Taliban with the dark sunglasses turns out to be ___________.

II. SHORT ANSWER

1. What does it mean to "run" a kite?

2. Why does Amir want to win the kite tournament so badly?

3. What happens to Hassan after he has caught the last fallen kite from the tournament?

4. Why does Amir compare the look in Hassan's eyes while Assef is hurting him to the look in the lamb's eyes before it is killed for food?

5. Amir and his father are enjoying their new relationship until Amir asks him a question that angers him. What is this question?

6. What does Amir do to get Ali and Hassan in trouble?

7. How do Amir and his father travel on the second leg of their trip to safety?

8. How did the people of Afghanistan react when the Taliban took control of the country?

9. What shocking news does Rahim tell Amir?

10. Why does Farid try to kill the director of the orphanage?

11. What does Amir have to do to "earn" Sohrab?

12. Describe how Amir is finally able to leave the room and get away to safety with Sohrab.

13. What is the significance of Amir's injury to his lip?

14. What did Sohrab do to himself?

15. Describe how Sohrab acts once in America.

III. ESSAY

1. How does the author use events from history in the novel? What does this add to the story?

2. What is the significance of the phrase, "for you a thousand times over"? How is it used throughout the novel?

IV. Vocabulary

A. Write the vocabulary words you are given. After writing them down, go back and write in their definitions.

Word	Definition
1	
2	
3	
4	
5	
6	
7	
8	
9	
10	

The Kite Runner SHORT ANSWER UNIT TEST 2 Answer Key

I. MATCHING/IDENTIFY

F	1. RAHIM	A. He smuggles people out of Afghanistan to safety in Pakistan.
S	2. FACE	B. Ali is killed by stepping on one of these.
C	3. LIP	C. Hassan is born with a deformity on his __________.
I	4. THEFT	D. Amir, his father, and several other people wait here while the truck is repaired to go to Pakistan.
K	5. KNUCKLES	E. Weapon used by both Hassan and Sohrab to save Amir
H	6. HITLER	F. Best friend and business partner to Amir's father
E	7. SLINGSHOT	G. Soraya's ________ is able to help get Sohrab into America.
L	8. LAST	H. Person Assef idolizes
P	9. GLASS	I. Amir's father believes ____ is the root of all other sins.
A	10. KARIM	J. Soraya's chosen profession
D	11. BASEMENT	K. Assef is known for carrying around brass _____________.
J	12. TEACHER	L. The __________ kite to fall is the most coveted by kite runners.
Q	13. AUTHOR	M. Place where Hassan was shot and killed
R	14. PREGNANT	N. Amir works to raise money for a _________ in Afghanistan.
B	15. MINE	O. Sohrab takes a long one of these each night before he goes to bed.
M	16. STREET	P. This is on the spool of the kite to help with kite fighting.
T	17. ASSEF	Q. Amir's chosen career
O	18. BATH	R. Despite how hard she tried, Soraya could not get ____________.
G	19. UNCLE	S. Ali's ______ and leg are both crippled/paralyzed.
N	20. HOSPITAL	T. The man in the Taliban with the dark sunglasses turns out to be ___________.

II. SHORT ANSWER

1. What does it mean to "run" a kite?
   A kite runner is someone who runs all around the city trying to catch a falling kite before it lands.
2. Why does Amir want to win the kite tournament so badly?
   Amir realizes this is a way to gain his father's love and affection and to finally make him proud.
3. What happens to Hassan after he has caught the last fallen kite from the tournament?
   He is raped by Assef.
4. Why does Amir compare the look in Hassan's eyes while Assef is hurting him to the look in the lamb's eyes before it is killed for food?
   Both have a look of acceptance and understanding of the situation and are resigned to enduring it for a higher purpose.
5. Amir and his father are enjoying their new relationship until Amir asks him a question that angers him. What is this question?
   Amir asks his father if he's ever thought of getting new servants.
6. What does Amir do to get Ali and Hassan in trouble?
   Amir hides his new watch and some money under Hassan's mattress to make it look like he was stealing from them.
7. How do Amir and his father travel on the second leg of their trip to safety?
   They are put into an empty fuel tank with several others. There is absolutely no light, the air they breathe is full of gasoline fumes, and they cannot move or get out for quite some time.
8. How did the people of Afghanistan react when the Taliban took control of the country?
   They were happy, they celebrated and danced in the streets because they thought it was an end to the war and their country would once again know peace.
9. What shocking news does Rahim tell Amir?
   Rahim explains that Ali was sterile and could not have children. He then alludes to the fact that Amir's father was also Hassan's father. He had gotten Hassan's mother pregnant so Ali could have a child, and they kept it a secret all this time. Amir and Hassan were actually half brothers.
10. Why does Farid try to kill the director of the orphanage?
    He finds out that he is selling children for sexual purposes to the Taliban. This outrages him, and he jumps on the director and nearly kills him until Amir tells him the children are watching.
11. What does Amir have to do to "earn" Sohrab?
    He has to fight Assef. Assef reminds him they have unfinished business from when they were children, and in order to leave they must fight until one of them is killed.
12. Describe how Amir is finally able to leave the room and get away to safety with Sohrab.
    Sohrab picks up a brass ball off the bottom of the table and puts it in his slingshot. He asks Assef to stop, and when he doesn't he shoots him in the eye. Assef loses his eye and is in great pain.
13. What is the significance of Amir's injury to his lip?
    Hassan was harelipped and had a scar in the same place above his mouth. Now, Amir has the same exact scar that Hassan had.
14. What did Sohrab do to himself?
    He used Amir's razor blade to try to commit suicide.

15. Describe how Sohrab acts once in America.
Sohrab is silent. He never speaks to anyone and takes up very little space. He sleeps all the time and sometimes it is hard to remember he is even there.

IV. Vocabulary

A. Write the vocabulary words you are given. After writing them down, go back and write in their definitions.

Word	Definition
1	
2	
3	
4	
5	
6	
7	
8	
9	
10	

Select the vocabulary words for Short Answer Test 2

The Kite Runner ADVANCED SHORT ANSWER TEST

I. MATCHING/IDENTIFY

____ 1.	RAHIM	A.	Amir's chosen career
____ 2.	FACE	B.	Assef is known for carrying around brass ____________.
____ 3.	LIP	C.	Best friend and business partner to Amir's father
____ 4.	THEFT	D.	Ali's ______ and leg are both crippled/paralyzed.
____ 5.	KNUCKLES	E.	He smuggles people out of Afghanistan to safety in Pakistan.
____ 6.	HITLER	F.	Place where Hassan was shot and killed
____ 7.	SLINGSHOT	G.	This is on the spool of the kite to help with kite fighting.
____ 8.	LAST	H.	Weapon used by both Hassan and Sohrab to save Amir
____ 9.	GLASS	I.	Ali is killed by stepping on one of these.
____ 10.	KARIM	J.	Soraya's ________ is able to help get Sohrab into America.
____ 11.	BASEMENT	K.	Despite how hard she tried, Soraya could not get ___________.
____ 12.	TEACHER	L.	The __________ kite to fall is the most coveted by kite runners.
____ 13.	AUTHOR	M.	Amir works to raise money for a _________ in Afghanistan.
____ 14.	PREGNANT	N.	Sohrab takes a long one of these each night before he goes to bed.
____ 15.	MINE	O.	Person Assef idolizes
____ 16.	STREET	P.	Hassan is born with a deformity on his __________.
____ 17.	ASSEF	Q.	Amir's father believes ____ is the root of all other sins.
____ 18.	BATH	R.	Amir, his father, and several other people wait here while the truck is repaired to go to Pakistan.
____ 19.	UNCLE	S.	Soraya's chosen profession
____ 20.	HOSPITAL	T.	The man in the Taliban with the dark sunglasses turns out to be ___________.

II. SHORT ANSWER

1. How does the author use events from history in the novel? What does this add to the story?

2. What is the significance of what Amir reads about Hassan's people, the Hazaras, and his own people, the Pashtuns?

3. How are Amir and Hassan's first words important?

4. After Hassan has surgery to fix his cleft lip (that looks like a permanent smile) Amir says, "The swelling subsided, and the wound healed with time. Soon, it was just a pink jagged line running up from his lip. By the following winter, it was only a faint scar. Which was ironic. Because that was the winter that Hassan stopped smiling." What reasons does Hassan have to stop smiling?

5. Amir says, 'I actually aspired to cowardice, because the alternative, the real reason I was running, was that Assef was right: Nothing is free in this world. Maybe Hassan was the price I had to pay, the lamb I had to slay, to win Baba.' How does Amir rationalize running away from his friend as he is being raped in the alley?

6. Amir says, "I understood the nature of my new curse: I was going to get away with it." What does he mean by this statement?

7. Compare and contrast the different ways Amir and his father view America.

8. Amir and his father don't see eye to eye on Amir's college plans. Why is it so important for Amir to stand his ground and major in English like he plans?

9. Why is Amir so understanding of Soraya's past? Why doesn't he care about the shameful things she has done?

10. What did Amir's father steal from him by lying about Hassan?

11. Amir says, "Baba and I were more alike than I'd ever known. We had both betrayed the people who would have given their lives for us. And with that came this realization: that Rahim Khan had summoned me here to atone not just for my sins but for Baba's too." What does he mean by this statement?

12. As Amir is getting beaten to near death by Assef he says, "for the first time since the winter of 1975, I felt at peace." What does he mean by this?

13. Explain the irony of the situation when Sohrab hits Assef in the eye with a slingshot, saving Amir.

14. How are Soraya's expectations about having Sohrab as a son different from reality?

15. What is the significance of the phrase, "for you a thousand times over"? How is it used throughout the novel?

16. How does the author leave the reader with a sense of hope at the end of the novel?

III. ESSAY

1. How does the author break American stereotypes of Afghanistan in this novel?

2. How does the author incorporate both guilt and atonement in the novel? What was he trying to say about both of these feelings?

IV. Vocabulary

A. Write the vocabulary words you are given. After writing them down, go back and write in their definitions.

Word	Definition
1	
2	
3	
4	
5	
6	
7	
8	
9	
10	

The Kite Runner ADVANCED SHORT ANSWER TEST Answer Key

I. MATCHING/IDENTIFY

C	1. RAHIM	A. Amir's chosen career
D	2. FACE	B. Assef is known for carrying around brass ____________.
P	3. LIP	C. Best friend and business partner to Amir's father
Q	4. THEFT	D. Ali's ______ and leg are both crippled/paralyzed.
B	5. KNUCKLES	E. He smuggles people out of Afghanistan to safety in Pakistan.
O	6. HITLER	F. Place where Hassan was shot and killed
H	7. SLINGSHOT	G. This is on the spool of the kite to help with kite fighting.
L	8. LAST	H. Weapon used by both Hassan and Sohrab to save Amir
G	9. GLASS	I. Ali is killed by stepping on one of these.
E	10. KARIM	J. Soraya's ________ is able to help get Sohrab into America.
R	11. BASEMENT	K. Despite how hard she tried, Soraya could not get ____________.
S	12. TEACHER	L. The __________ kite to fall is the most coveted by kite runners.
A	13. AUTHOR	M. Amir works to raise money for a _________ in Afghanistan.
K	14. PREGNANT	N. Sohrab takes a long one of these each night before he goes to bed.
I	15. MINE	O. Person Assef idolizes
F	16. STREET	P. Hassan is born with a deformity on his __________.
T	17. ASSEF	Q. Amir's father believes ____ is the root of all other sins.
N	18. BATH	R. Amir, his father, and several other people wait here while the truck is repaired to go to Pakistan.
J	19. UNCLE	S. Soraya's chosen profession
M	20. HOSPITAL	T. The man in the Taliban with the dark sunglasses turns out to be ___________.

IV. Vocabulary

A. Write the vocabulary words you are given. After writing them down, go back and write in their definitions.

Word	Definition
1	
2	
3	
4	
5	
6	
7	
8	
9	
10	

Select the vocabulary words for the Advanced Short Answer Test

The Kite Runner MULTIPLE CHOICE TEST 1

I. MATCHING/IDENTIFY

____ 1.	RAHIM	A.	The __________ kite to fall is the most coveted by kite runners.
____ 2.	FACE	B.	Despite how hard she tried, Soraya could not get ____________.
____ 3.	LIP	C.	Amir's chosen career
____ 4.	THEFT	D.	Amir's father believes ____ is the root of all other sins.
____ 5.	KNUCKLES	E.	Weapon used by both Hassan and Sohrab to save Amir
____ 6.	HITLER	F.	He smuggles people out of Afghanistan to safety in Pakistan.
____ 7.	SLINGSHOT	G.	Ali is killed by stepping on one of these.
____ 8.	LAST	H.	Best friend and business partner to Amir's father
____ 9.	GLASS	I.	Person Assef idolizes
____ 10.	KARIM	J.	Ali's ______ and leg are both crippled/paralyzed.
____ 11.	BASEMENT	K.	Hassan is born with a deformity on his __________.
____ 12.	TEACHER	L.	Amir, his father, and several other people wait here while the truck is repaired to go to Pakistan.
____ 13.	AUTHOR	M.	Place where Hassan was shot and killed
____ 14.	PREGNANT	N.	Amir works to raise money for a _________ in Afghanistan.
____ 15.	MINE	O.	This is on the spool of the kite to help with kite fighting.
____ 16.	STREET	P.	Assef is known for carrying around brass _____________.
____ 17.	ASSEF	Q.	Soraya's chosen profession
____ 18.	BATH	R.	The man in the Taliban with the dark sunglasses turns out to be ___________.
____ 19.	UNCLE	S.	Sohrab takes a long one of these each night before he goes to bed.
____ 20.	HOSPITAL	T.	Soraya's ________ is able to help get Sohrab into America.

II. MULTIPLE CHOICE

1. What is the significance of Amir's injury to his lip?
   A. Amir has the same scar that Sohrab has, making them look like father and son.
   B. Amir will no longer be able to smile, just like Hassan did not smile in all those years he suffered from what happened after the kite tournament.
   C. Amir will no longer be able to speak normally, making him sound even less American when he returns home to the United States.
   D. Amir has the same scar that Hassan had with his harelip.

2. How did Amir's family come to know Ali?
   A. Ali's parents were hit by impaired drivers. The drivers were brought before Amir's grandfather, the judge, along with the orphaned son, Ali. After the trial, Amir's grandfather adopted Ali, and he was raised alongside Amir's father.
   B. Ali's parents were arrested for aiding the government. Amir's grandfather handled the court case and sentenced them to death. He felt sorry for their son, who was not involved, and adopted Ali, who was raised alongside Amir's father.
   C. Ali's parents were very poor and could not afford to feed and house their son. Each day, they watched as Amir's grandfather walked out of the courthouse and to his expensive car. One day they stopped him and begged him to take Hassan, who was then raised alongside Amir's father.
   D. Ali's parents were very wealthy and traveled for business quite often. They constantly left Hassan home alone and one day decided to send him to live with his good friend from school, Amir's father. He ended up living with them and the two were raised together.

3. What does it mean to "run" a kite?
   A. A kite runner is someone who helps the flyer get the kite in the air by running until the wind catches it.
   B. A kite runner is someone who has won at least three fighting tournaments.
   C. A kite runner is someone who runs all around the city trying to catch a falling kite before it lands.
   D. A kite runner is someone who sells fighting kites to people to enter in the tournament.

4. Why does Amir want to win the kite tournament so badly?
   A. Amir realizes this is a way to gain his father's love and affection and finally make him proud.
   B. Amir thinks this will help him win the attention of girls.
   C. Amir really wants to win the $1000 prize so he can buy more books.
   D. Amir believes this is the best way for he and Hassan to become better friends.

5. What happens to Hassan after he has caught the last fallen tournament kite?
   A. He is raped by Assef.
   B. He is granted a kiss from a mysterious girl.
   C. He is stabbed in a fight for possession of the kite.
   D. He is awared $50 from Amir for getting him the kite.

6. Describe Amir's relationship with his father after winning the kiten tournament.
   A. He and his father spend a lot of money. His father takes Amir with him to by a new sports car, Amir gets new "American" clothes, and they buy a color TV for Amir's bedroom.
   B. He and his father spend a lot of time together. His father takes Amir to the movies, they visit the zoo, and go on trips.
   C. He and his father are still not that close. Though Amir's father brags about Amir's win to others, he still doesn't talk to Amir at dinner, and he often goes to his study to be alone.
   D. He and his father do everything together. His father takes Amir with him to work to show off his son who won the tournament, also, Amir's father invites Amir to sit with him and Rahim in the study as they smoke cigars in the evening.

7. How does Amir's father react when Ali quits?
   A. He refuses to pay them for the last month
   B. He hurries them out of the house so no one will know
   C. He begs them not to leave and cries
   D. He laughs and tells him he was already fired

8. How do Amir and his father travel on the second leg of their trip to safety?
   A. They must hike through steep, mountainous areas where there are no checkpoints since travel in this area is so dangerous. They deal with sand storms and harsh winds, nearly dying from the weather conditions.
   B. They must crawl through an intricate tunnel system. There is no light, and they must crawl for days, unable to stand or stretch, with no food and minimal water.
   C. They are put into an empty fuel tank with several others. There is absolutely no light, the air they breathe is full of gasoline fumes, and they cannot move or get out for quite some time.
   D. They lie on a pile of bodies being taken to burial. They have to remain still and endure the awful stench of rotting bodies as they travel across the border.

9. What shocking news does Rahim tell Amir?
   A. That Amir's mother is also Hassan's mother; they are half brothers
   B. That Amir's mother gave birth to twins, but one was sent away since they could not afford to care for two children
   C. That Amir's father is also Hassan's father; they are half brothers
   D. That Amir's parents could not have children; Amir is adopted

10. How did the people of Afghanistan react when the Taliban took control of the country?
   A. They were worried about the state of the country and many fled for safety elsewhere.
   B. They were so upset many rioted and protested in the streets.
   C. They were so happy they celebrated and danced in the streets.
   D. They were overjoyed and offered gifts of joy to the Taliban as they moved in to the city.

11. What does the director of the orphanage say happened to Sohrab?
   A. Sohrab had special needs and was sent to an orphanage that could provide him with the medical care he needed.
   B. The Taliban came in shooting Hazara children. Sohrab was able to escape and has not been heard of since.
   C. A man from the Taliban occasionally comes to take a child for his personal pleasure. Sohrab was the child he chose to take the last time.
   D. The kids all made fun of Sohrab and beat him up repeatedly. Sohrab fought back injuring four kids with his slingshot and ran away.

12. What happens at half-time during the soccer game?
   A. A popular musician plays patriotic music as people dance in the aisle
   B. Amir meets with the man who knows of Sohrab's whereabouts
   C. The Taliban stones two people to death
   D. The crowd takes a break for afternoon prayer

13. Why does Amir start laughing when he is in so much pain?

   A. He hits a breaking point from the pain where his mind and body begin to shut down. All he can do is laugh until he is almost hysterical and can no longer feel the pain.
   B. He realizes that for the first time since the winter of 1975 he was at peace, even though he was getting severely beaten.
   C. He cannot believe how things have worked out in his life. He can't help but laugh at the irony of the situation.
   D. He understands that this is the punishment he must receive in order to be cleared of his sins and live a peaceful afterlife, which makes him laugh at God's twisted sense of humor.

14. Describe how Amir is finally able to leave the room and get away to safety with Sohrab.

   A. Amir is beaten so severely he goes into shock. The man from the Taliban thinks this comatose state is actually death, and leaves Amir to die in the room. Sohrab is left alone in the room and notices a faint breathing coming from Amir. He then waits until night to drag Amir's body outside where Farid is waiting with the car.
   B. Sohrab takes a knife he had hidden in his waistband and stabs the man from the Taliban. This does not kill him but stuns him long enough for Amir to pull the knife out and stab him in the heart, killing him and allowing them to leave.
   C. Amir gives up and allows the man to beat him to near death. The man from the Taliban gets angry that Amir is laughing at him and not fighting back and throws him out of the room to die. Farid sees this and hurries to take him to safety.
   D. Sohrab finds a brass ball and shoots the man from the Taliban in the eye with his slingshot.

15. What happens at the celebration Amir and his family attend that makes Sohrab smile?

   A. He meets another orphan from Afghanistan who has experienced many of the same conditions he did.
   B. He flies a kite with Amir. The two fight another kite and win.
   C. He tries a glass of wine, and it makes him remember feasting with his father.
   D. He sees a framed picture of Amir and Hassan along with their favorite children's book.

III. VOCABULARY

_____ 1.	NOTORIOUSLY	A.	Relieving or soothing the symptoms of a disease or disorder without affecting a cure
_____ 2.	UNSCRUPULOUS	B.	Sincere; honest; straightforward
_____ 3.	VALIANT	C.	Having no conscience or principles; oblivious to what is right or honorable
_____ 4.	TREPIDATION	D.	Characterized by having no useful result; uselessness
_____ 5.	GUILELESS	E.	Deep and painful regret for wrongdoing
_____ 6.	CHASM	F.	Boldly courageous; brave
_____ 7.	LUCRATIVE	G.	Causing sorrow or pity; deplorable; mournful
_____ 8.	RUEFUL	H.	Exemption from punishment, penalty, or harm
_____ 9.	INSINUATION	I.	Dealing or concerned with facts or actual occurrences; practical
_____ 10.	PALLIATIVE	J.	To make amends, as for a sin or fault
_____ 11.	FUTILITY	K.	An indirect or covert suggestion or hint especially of a derogatory nature
_____ 12.	PRAGMATIC	L.	A state of alarm or dread; apprehension
_____ 13.	UNREQUITED	M.	A pronounced difference of opinion, interests, or loyalty
_____ 14.	ATONE	N.	Requiring great exertion; laborious; difficult
_____ 15.	ARDUOUS	O.	Known widely and usually unfavorably known
_____ 16.	PRUDENCE	P.	Foul and repulsive, as from lack of care or cleanliness; neglected and filthy
_____ 17.	REMORSE	Q.	Caution with regard to practical matters; regard for one's own interests
_____ 18.	SURREAL	R.	Having the disorienting, hallucinatory quality of a dream; seeming unreal; fantastic
_____ 19.	IMPUNITY	S.	Profitable; moneymaking
_____ 20.	SQUALID	T.	Not returned or reciprocated

IV. ESSAY

1. What is the significance of the phrase, "for you a thousand times over"? How is it used throughout the novel?

2. How does the author leave the reader with a sense of hope at the end of the novel?

The Kite Runner MULTIPLE CHOICE TEST 1 Answer Key

I. MATCHING/IDENTIFY

H	1. RAHIM	A. The __________ kite to fall is the most coveted by kite runners.
J	2. FACE	B. Despite how hard she tried, Soraya could not get ____________.
K	3. LIP	C. Amir's chosen career
D	4. THEFT	D. Amir's father believes ____ is the root of all other sins.
P	5. KNUCKLES	E. Weapon used by both Hassan and Sohrab to save Amir
I	6. HITLER	F. He smuggles people out of Afghanistan to safety in Pakistan.
E	7. SLINGSHOT	G. Ali is killed by stepping on one of these.
A	8. LAST	H. Best friend and business partner to Amir's father
O	9. GLASS	I. Person Assef idolizes
F	10. KARIM	J. Ali's ______ and leg are both crippled/paralyzed.
L	11. BASEMENT	K. Hassan is born with a deformity on his __________.
Q	12. TEACHER	L. Amir, his father, and several other people wait here while the truck is repaired to go to Pakistan.
C	13. AUTHOR	M. Place where Hassan was shot and killed
B	14. PREGNANT	N. Amir works to raise money for a _________ in Afghanistan.
G	15. MINE	O. This is on the spool of the kite to help with kite fighting.
M	16. STREET	P. Assef is known for carrying around brass ____________.
R	17. ASSEF	Q. Soraya's chosen profession
S	18. BATH	R. The man in the Taliban with the dark sunglasses turns out to be ___________.
T	19. UNCLE	S. Sohrab takes a long one of these each night before he goes to bed.
N	20. HOSPITAL	T. Soraya's ________ is able to help get Sohrab into America.

II. MULTIPLE CHOICE

D 1. What is the significance of Amir's injury to his lip?

A. Amir has the same scar that Sohrab has, making them look like father and son.

B. Amir will no longer be able to smile, just like Hassan did not smile in all those years he suffered from what happened after the kite tournament.

C. Amir will no longer be able to speak normally, making him sound even less American when he returns home to the United States.

D. Amir has the same scar that Hassan had with his harelip.

A 2. How did Amir's family come to know Ali?

A. Ali's parents were hit by impaired drivers. The drivers were brought before Amir's grandfather, the judge, along with the orphaned son, Ali. After the trial, Amir's grandfather adopted Ali, and he was raised alongside Amir's father.

B. Ali's parents were arrested for aiding the government. Amir's grandfather handled the court case and sentenced them to death. He felt sorry for their son, who was not involved, and adopted Ali, who was raised alongside Amir's father.

C. Ali's parents were very poor and could not afford to feed and house their son. Each day, they watched as Amir's grandfather walked out of the courthouse and to his expensive car. One day they stopped him and begged him to take Hassan, who was then raised alongside Amir's father.

D. Ali's parents were very wealthy and traveled for business quite often. They constantly left Hassan home alone and one day decided to send him to live with his good friend from school, Amir's father. He ended up living with them and the two were raised together.

C 3. What does it mean to "run" a kite?

A. A kite runner is someone who helps the flyer get the kite in the air by running until the wind catches it.

B. A kite runner is someone who has won at least three fighting tournaments.

C. A kite runner is someone who runs all around the city trying to catch a falling kite before it lands.

D. A kite runner is someone who sells fighting kites to people to enter in the tournament.

A 4. Why does Amir want to win the kite tournament so badly?

A. Amir realizes this is a way to gain his father's love and affection and finally make him proud.

B. Amir thinks this will help him win the attention of girls.

C. Amir really wants to win the $1000 prize so he can buy more books.

D. Amir believes this is the best way for he and Hassan to become better friends.

A 5. What happens to Hassan after he has caught the last fallen tournament kite?

A. He is raped by Assef.

B. He is granted a kiss from a mysterious girl.

C. He is stabbed in a fight for possession of the kite.

D. He is awared $50 from Amir for getting him the kite.

B 6. Describe Amir's relationship with his father after winning the kiten tournament.

A. He and his father spend a lot of money. His father takes Amir with him to by a new sports car, Amir gets new "American" clothes, and they buy a color TV for Amir's bedroom.

B. He and his father spend a lot of time together. His father takes Amir to the movies, they visit the zoo, and go on trips.

C. He and his father are still not that close. Though Amir's father brags about Amir's win to others, he still doesn't talk to Amir at dinner, and he often goes to his study to be alone.

D. He and his father do everything together. His father takes Amir with him to work to show off his son who won the tournament, also, Amir's father invites Amir to sit with him and Rahim in the study as they smoke cigars in the evening.

C 7. How does Amir's father react when Ali quits?

A. He refuses to pay them for the last month

B. He hurries them out of the house so no one will know

C. He begs them not to leave and cries

D. He laughs and tells him he was already fired

C 8. How do Amir and his father travel on the second leg of their trip to safety?

A. They must hike through steep, mountainous areas where there are no checkpoints since travel in this area is so dangerous. They deal with sand storms and harsh winds, nearly dying from the weather conditions.

B. They must crawl through an intricate tunnel system. There is no light, and they must crawl for days, unable to stand or stretch, with no food and minimal water.

C. They are put into an empty fuel tank with several others. There is absolutely no light, the air they breathe is full of gasoline fumes, and they cannot move or get out for quite some time.

D. They lie on a pile of bodies being taken to burial. They have to remain still and endure the awful stench of rotting bodies as they travel across the border.

C 9. What shocking news does Rahim tell Amir?

A. That Amir's mother is also Hassan's mother; they are half brothers

B. That Amir's mother gave birth to twins, but one was sent away since they could not afford to care for two children

C. That Amir's father is also Hassan's father; they are half brothers

D. That Amir's parents could not have children; Amir is adopted

C 10. How did the people of Afghanistan react when the Taliban took control of the country?

A. They were worried about the state of the country and many fled for safety elsewhere.

B. They were so upset many rioted and protested in the streets.

C. They were so happy they celebrated and danced in the streets.

D. They were overjoyed and offered gifts of joy to the Taliban as they moved in to the city.

C 11. What does the director of the orphanage say happened to Sohrab?

A. Sohrab had special needs and was sent to an orphanage that could provide him with the medical care he needed.

B. The Taliban came in shooting Hazara children. Sohrab was able to escape and has not been heard of since.

C. A man from the Taliban occasionally comes to take a child for his personal pleasure. Sohrab was the child he chose to take the last time.

D. The kids all made fun of Sohrab and beat him up repeatedly. Sohrab fought back injuring four kids with his slingshot and ran away.

C 12. What happens at half-time during the soccer game?

A. A popular musician plays patriotic music as people dance in the aisle

B. Amir meets with the man who knows of Sohrab's whereabouts

C. The Taliban stones two people to death

D. The crowd takes a break for afternoon prayer

B 13. Why does Amir start laughing when he is in so much pain?

A. He hits a breaking point from the pain where his mind and body begin to shut down. All he can do is laugh until he is almost hysterical and can no longer feel the pain.

B. He realizes that for the first time since the winter of 1975 he was at peace, even though he was getting severely beaten.

C. He cannot believe how things have worked out in his life. He can't help but laugh at the irony of the situation.

D. He understands that this is the punishment he must receive in order to be cleared of his sins and live a peaceful afterlife, which makes him laugh at God's twisted sense of humor.

D 14. Describe how Amir is finally able to leave the room and get away to safety with Sohrab.

A. Amir is beaten so severely he goes into shock. The man from the Taliban thinks this comatose state is actually death, and leaves Amir to die in the room. Sohrab is left alone in the room and notices a faint breathing coming from Amir. He then waits until night to drag Amir's body outside where Farid is waiting with the car.

B. Sohrab takes a knife he had hidden in his waistband and stabs the man from the Taliban. This does not kill him but stuns him long enough for Amir to pull the knife out and stab him in the heart, killing him and allowing them to leave.

C. Amir gives up and allows the man to beat him to near death. The man from the Taliban gets angry that Amir is laughing at him and not fighting back and throws him out of the room to die. Farid sees this and hurries to take him to safety.

D. Sohrab finds a brass ball and shoots the man from the Taliban in the eye with his slingshot.

B 15. What happens at the celebration Amir and his family attend that makes Sohrab smile?

A. He meets another orphan from Afghanistan who has experienced many of the same conditions he did.

B. He flies a kite with Amir. The two fight another kite and win.

C. He tries a glass of wine, and it makes him remember feasting with his father.

D. He sees a framed picture of Amir and Hassan along with their favorite children's book.

III. VOCABULARY

O	1. NOTORIOUSLY	A. Relieving or soothing the symptoms of a disease or disorder without affecting a cure
C	2. UNSCRUPULOUS	B. Sincere; honest; straightforward
F	3. VALIANT	C. Having no conscience or principles; oblivious to what is right or honorable
L	4. TREPIDATION	D. Characterized by having no useful result; uselessness
B	5. GUILELESS	E. Deep and painful regret for wrongdoing
M	6. CHASM	F. Boldly courageous; brave
S	7. LUCRATIVE	G. Causing sorrow or pity; deplorable; mournful
G	8. RUEFUL	H. Exemption from punishment, penalty, or harm
K	9. INSINUATION	I. Dealing or concerned with facts or actual occurrences; practical
A	10. PALLIATIVE	J. To make amends, as for a sin or fault
D	11. FUTILITY	K. An indirect or covert suggestion or hint especially of a derogatory nature
I	12. PRAGMATIC	L. A state of alarm or dread; apprehension
T	13. UNREQUITED	M. A pronounced difference of opinion, interests, or loyalty
J	14. ATONE	N. Requiring great exertion; laborious; difficult
N	15. ARDUOUS	O. Known widely and usually unfavorably known
Q	16. PRUDENCE	P. Foul and repulsive, as from lack of care or cleanliness; neglected and filthy
E	17. REMORSE	Q. Caution with regard to practical matters; regard for one's own interests
R	18. SURREAL	R. Having the disorienting, hallucinatory quality of a dream; seeming unreal; fantastic
H	19. IMPUNITY	S. Profitable; moneymaking
P	20. SQUALID	T. Not returned or reciprocated

The Kite Runner MULTIPLE CHOICE TEST 2

I. MATCHING/IDENTIFY

____	1.	RAHIM	A.	Amir's chosen career
____	2.	FACE	B.	Soraya's ________ is able to help get Sohrab into America.
____	3.	LIP	C.	Ali's ______ and leg are both crippled/paralyzed.
____	4.	THEFT	D.	He smuggles people out of Afghanistan to safety in Pakistan.
____	5.	KNUCKLES	E.	Place where Hassan was shot and killed
____	6.	HITLER	F.	Sohrab takes a long one of these each night before he goes to bed.
____	7.	SLINGSHOT	G.	Amir, his father, and several other people wait here while the truck is repaired to go to Pakistan.
____	8.	LAST	H.	Ali is killed by stepping on one of these.
____	9.	GLASS	I.	Amir's father believes ____ is the root of all other sins.
____	10.	KARIM	J.	Best friend and business partner to Amir's father
____	11.	BASEMENT	K.	Soraya's chosen profession
____	12.	TEACHER	L.	Hassan is born with a deformity on his _________.
____	13.	AUTHOR	M.	Assef is known for carrying around brass ____________.
____	14.	PREGNANT	N.	The man in the Taliban with the dark sunglasses turns out to be ___________.
____	15.	MINE	O.	The __________ kite to fall is the most coveted by kite runners.
____	16.	STREET	P.	This is on the spool of the kite to help with kite fighting.
____	17.	ASSEF	Q.	Person Assef idolizes
____	18.	BATH	R.	Weapon used by both Hassan and Sohrab to save Amir
____	19.	UNCLE	S.	Amir works to raise money for a _________ in Afghanistan.
____	20.	HOSPITAL	T.	Despite how hard she tried, Soraya could not get ____________.

II. MULTIPLE CHOICE

1. What does it mean to "run" a kite?
   A. A kite runner is someone who runs all around the city trying to catch a falling kite before it lands.
   B. A kite runner is someone who helps the flyer get the kite in the air by running until the wind catches it.
   C. A kite runner is someone who has won at least three fighting tournaments.
   D. A kite runner is someone who sells fighting kites to people to enter in the tournament.

2. Describe how Sohrab acts once in America.
   A. He is talkative when it is just Amir, but hasn't warmed up to strangers.
   B. He is struggling to learn English but enjoys seeing California and experiencing new things.
   C. He is silent and sleeps a lot.
   D. He is making progress in learning English and has made a few friends in the neighborhood.

3. What is the significance of Amir's injury to his lip?
   A. Amir has the same scar that Hassan had with his harelip.
   B. Amir will no longer be able to speak normally, making him sound even less American when he returns home to the United States.
   C. Amir will no longer be able to smile, just like Hassan did not smile in all those years he suffered from what happened after the kite tournament.
   D. Amir has the same scar that Sohrab has, making them look like father and son.

4. Describe how Amir is finally able to leave the room and get away to safety with Sohrab.
   A. Sohrab takes a knife he had hidden in his waistband and stabs the man from the Taliban. This does not kill him but stuns him long enough for Amir to pull the knife out and stab him in the heart, killing him and allowing them to leave.
   B. Amir is beaten so severely he goes into shock. The man from the Taliban thinks this comatose state is actually death, and leaves Amir to die in the room. Sohrab is left alone in the room and notices a faint breathing coming from Amir. He then waits until night to drag Amir's body outside where Farid is waiting with the car.
   C. Sohrab finds a brass ball and shoots the man from the Taliban in the eye with his slingshot.
   D. Amir gives up and allows the man to beat him to near death. The man from the Taliban gets angry that Amir is laughing at him and not fighting back and throws him out of the room to die. Farid sees this and hurries to take him to safety.

5. Why does Farid try to kill the director of the orphanage?
   A. He is outraged that the man will not help them find Sohrab.
   B. He finds out he is allowing children to abuse each other physically.
   C. He is outraged that many children are starving and have no real beds to sleep in.
   D. He finds out that he is selling children for sexual purposes to the Taliban.

6. How did the people of Afghanistan react when the Taliban took control of the country?
   A. They were overjoyed and offered gifts of joy to the Taliban as they moved in to the city.
   B. They were so happy they celebrated and danced in the streets.
   C. They were so upset many rioted and protested in the streets.
   D. They were worried about the state of the country and many fled for safety elsewhere.

7. What shocking news does Rahim tell Amir?
   A. That Amir's father is also Hassan's father; they are half brothers
   B. That Amir's mother is also Hassan's mother; they are half brothers
   C. That Amir's parents could not have children; Amir is adopted
   D. That Amir's mother gave birth to twins, but one was sent away since they could not afford to care for two children

8. How do Amir and his father travel on the second leg of their trip to safety?
   A. They must hike through steep, mountainous areas where there are no checkpoints since travel in this area is so dangerous. They deal with sand storms and harsh winds, nearly dying from the weather conditions.
   B. They must crawl through an intricate tunnel system. There is no light, and they must crawl for days, unable to stand or stretch, with no food and minimal water.
   C. They lie on a pile of bodies being taken to burial. They have to remain still and endure the awful stench of rotting bodies as they travel across the border.
   D. They are put into an empty fuel tank with several others. There is absolutely no light, the air they breathe is full of gasoline fumes, and they cannot move or get out for quite some time.

9. What does Amir do to get Ali and Hassan in trouble?
   A. Amir goes around the house making a mess to make it look like Ali isn't able to do his job.
   B. Amir records Hassan making rude comments about Assef and tells his father he was disrespecting an honored family friend.
   C. Amir writes letters from a fake mistress addressed to Ali to make it look like Ali is unworthy of working in such a respected household.
   D. Amir hides his new watch and some money under Hassan's mattress to make it look like he was stealing from them.

10. Amir and his father are enjoying their new relationship until Amir asks him a question that angers him. What is this question?
    A. If he's ever thought of getting new servants
    B. If he's ever thought about moving to America
    C. If he's ever thought about getting remarried
    D. If he's ever thought about adopting Hassan

11. Why does Amir compare the look in Hassan's eyes while Assef is hurting him to the look in the lamb's eyes before it is killed for food?
    A. Both have a look of extreme sadness and pain that is hard for anyone watching to forget.
    B. Both have a look that is accusing others of guilt, making them feel remorse for what they are about to do.
    C. Both have a look of acceptance and understanding and are resigned to enduring it for a higher purpose.
    D. Both have a look of being completely unaware of what is about to happen.

12. What happens to Hassan after he has caught the last fallen tournament kite?
    A. He is awared $50 from Amir for getting him the kite.
    B. He is stabbed in a fight for possession of the kite.
    C. He is granted a kiss from a mysterious girl.
    D. He is raped by Assef.

13. Why does Amir want to win the kite tournament so badly?

   A. Amir believes this is the best way for he and Hassan to become better friends.

   B. Amir realizes this is a way to gain his father's love and affection and finally make him proud.

   C. Amir really wants to win the $1000 prize so he can buy more books.

   D. Amir thinks this will help him win the attention of girls.

14. What did Sohrab do to himself?

   A. He tried to drown himself in the tub to commit suicide.

   B. He used Amir's razor blade to try to commit suicide.

   C. He used a laundry line to hang himself to try to commit suicide.

   D. He electrocuted himself to try to commit suicide.

III. VOCABULARY

____ 1.	GARRULOUS	A.	Pleasantly easy to approach and to talk to; friendly; cordial; warmly polite
____ 2.	FEIGNED	B.	Not real; pretended
____ 3.	DEMISE	C.	A confused hand-to-hand fight or struggle among several people
____ 4.	VIGIL	D.	Degree to which something is appropriate
____ 5.	TENETS	E.	To find out for certain
____ 6.	RETICENCE	F.	A watch kept during normal sleeping hours
____ 7.	CHAGRIN	G.	A feeling of vexation, marked by disappointment or humiliation
____ 8.	NONCHALANTLY	H.	Freed from guilt or blame
____ 9.	APTNESS	I.	The act of employing to the greatest possible advantage
____ 10.	AFFABLE	J.	Characterized by keen awareness, sharp intelligence, and often a sense of the practical
____ 11.	ATONE	K.	Does a service or favor for
____ 12.	OBLIVION	L.	State of being reluctant or reserved
____ 13.	OBLIGES	M.	Coolly unconcerned, indifferent; casually
____ 14.	EXPLOITATION	N.	Giving up; surrendering
____ 15.	EPIPHANY	O.	To make amends, as for a sin or fault
____ 16.	ABSOLVE	P.	The state of being completely forgotten or unknown
____ 17.	SHREWD	Q.	A sudden perception of or insight into the reality or essential meaning of something, usually initiated by some simple or commonplace occurrence or experience
____ 18.	ASCERTAIN	R.	Opinions, doctrines, or principles held as being true by a person or especially by an organization
____ 19.	RELINQUISHMENT	S.	Death or decline
____ 20.	MELEE	T.	Excessively talkative in a rambling, roundabout manner, especially about trivial matters

IV. ESSAY

1. How does the author use events from history in the novel? What does this add to the story?

2. What is the significance of the phrase, "for you a thousand times over"? How is it used throughout the novel?

The Kite Runner MULTIPLE CHOICE TEST 2 Answer Key

I. MATCHING/IDENTIFY

J	1. RAHIM	A. Amir's chosen career
C	2. FACE	B. Soraya's ________ is able to help get Sohrab into America.
L	3. LIP	C. Ali's ______ and leg are both crippled/paralyzed.
I	4. THEFT	D. He smuggles people out of Afghanistan to safety in Pakistan.
M	5. KNUCKLES	E. Place where Hassan was shot and killed
Q	6. HITLER	F. Sohrab takes a long one of these each night before he goes to bed.
R	7. SLINGSHOT	G. Amir, his father, and several other people wait here while the truck is repaired to go to Pakistan.
O	8. LAST	H. Ali is killed by stepping on one of these.
P	9. GLASS	I. Amir's father believes ____ is the root of all other sins.
D	10. KARIM	J. Best friend and business partner to Amir's father
G	11. BASEMENT	K. Soraya's chosen profession
K	12. TEACHER	L. Hassan is born with a deformity on his __________.
A	13. AUTHOR	M. Assef is known for carrying around brass _____________.
T	14. PREGNANT	N. The man in the Taliban with the dark sunglasses turns out to be ___________.
H	15. MINE	O. The __________ kite to fall is the most coveted by kite runners.
E	16. STREET	P. This is on the spool of the kite to help with kite fighting.
N	17. ASSEF	Q. Person Assef idolizes
F	18. BATH	R. Weapon used by both Hassan and Sohrab to save Amir
B	19. UNCLE	S. Amir works to raise money for a _________ in Afghanistan.
S	20. HOSPITAL	T. Despite how hard she tried, Soraya could not get ____________.

II. MULTIPLE CHOICE

A 1. What does it mean to "run" a kite?

A. A kite runner is someone who runs all around the city trying to catch a falling kite before it lands.

B. A kite runner is someone who helps the flyer get the kite in the air by running until the wind catches it.

C. A kite runner is someone who has won at least three fighting tournaments.

D. A kite runner is someone who sells fighting kites to people to enter in the tournament.

C 2. Describe how Sohrab acts once in America.

A. He is talkative when it is just Amir, but hasn't warmed up to strangers.

B. He is struggling to learn English but enjoys seeing California and experiencing new things.

C. He is silent and sleeps a lot.

D. He is making progress in learning English and has made a few friends in the neighborhood.

A 3. What is the significance of Amir's injury to his lip?

A. Amir has the same scar that Hassan had with his harelip.

B. Amir will no longer be able to speak normally, making him sound even less American when he returns home to the United States.

C. Amir will no longer be able to smile, just like Hassan did not smile in all those years he suffered from what happened after the kite tournament.

D. Amir has the same scar that Sohrab has, making them look like father and son.

C 4. Describe how Amir is finally able to leave the room and get away to safety with Sohrab.

A. Sohrab takes a knife he had hidden in his waistband and stabs the man from the Taliban. This does not kill him but stuns him long enough for Amir to pull the knife out and stab him in the heart, killing him and allowing them to leave.

B. Amir is beaten so severely he goes into shock. The man from the Taliban thinks this comatose state is actually death, and leaves Amir to die in the room. Sohrab is left alone in the room and notices a faint breathing coming from Amir. He then waits until night to drag Amir's body outside where Farid is waiting with the car.

C. Sohrab finds a brass ball and shoots the man from the Taliban in the eye with his slingshot.

D. Amir gives up and allows the man to beat him to near death. The man from the Taliban gets angry that Amir is laughing at him and not fighting back and throws him out of the room to die. Farid sees this and hurries to take him to safety.

D 5. Why does Farid try to kill the director of the orphanage?

A. He is outraged that the man will not help them find Sohrab.

B. He finds out he is allowing children to abuse each other physically.

C. He is outraged that many children are starving and have no real beds to sleep in.

D. He finds out that he is selling children for sexual purposes to the Taliban.

B 6. How did the people of Afghanistan react when the Taliban took control of the country?

A. They were overjoyed and offered gifts of joy to the Taliban as they moved in to the city.

B. They were so happy they celebrated and danced in the streets.

C. They were so upset many rioted and protested in the streets.

D. They were worried about the state of the country and many fled for safety elsewhere.

A 7. What shocking news does Rahim tell Amir?

A. That Amir's father is also Hassan's father; they are half brothers

B. That Amir's mother is also Hassan's mother; they are half brothers

C. That Amir's parents could not have children; Amir is adopted

D. That Amir's mother gave birth to twins, but one was sent away since they could not afford to care for two children

D 8. How do Amir and his father travel on the second leg of their trip to safety?

A. They must hike through steep, mountainous areas where there are no checkpoints since travel in this area is so dangerous. They deal with sand storms and harsh winds, nearly dying from the weather conditions.

B. They must crawl through an intricate tunnel system. There is no light, and they must crawl for days, unable to stand or stretch, with no food and minimal water.

C. They lie on a pile of bodies being taken to burial. They have to remain still and endure the awful stench of rotting bodies as they travel across the border.

D. They are put into an empty fuel tank with several others. There is absolutely no light, the air they breathe is full of gasoline fumes, and they cannot move or get out for quite some time.

D 9. What does Amir do to get Ali and Hassan in trouble?

A. Amir goes around the house making a mess to make it look like Ali isn't able to do his job.

B. Amir records Hassan making rude comments about Assef and tells his father he was disrespecting an honored family friend.

C. Amir writes letters from a fake mistress addressed to Ali to make it look like Ali is unworthy of working in such a respected household.

D. Amir hides his new watch and some money under Hassan's mattress to make it look like he was stealing from them.

A 10. Amir and his father are enjoying their new relationship until Amir asks him a question that angers him. What is this question?

A. If he's ever thought of getting new servants

B. If he's ever thought about moving to America

C. If he's ever thought about getting remarried

D. If he's ever thought about adopting Hassan

C 11. Why does Amir compare the look in Hassan's eyes while Assef is hurting him to the look in the lamb's eyes before it is killed for food?

A. Both have a look of extreme sadness and pain that is hard for anyone watching to forget.

B. Both have a look that is accusing others of guilt, making them feel remorse for what they are about to do.

C. Both have a look of acceptance and understanding and are resigned to enduring it for a higher purpose.

D. Both have a look of being completely unaware of what is about to happen.

D 12. What happens to Hassan after he has caught the last fallen tournament kite?

A. He is awared $50 from Amir for getting him the kite.

B. He is stabbed in a fight for possession of the kite.

C. He is granted a kiss from a mysterious girl.

D. He is raped by Assef.

B 13. Why does Amir want to win the kite tournament so badly?

A. Amir believes this is the best way for he and Hassan to become better friends.

B. Amir realizes this is a way to gain his father's love and affection and finally make him proud.

C. Amir really wants to win the $1000 prize so he can buy more books.

D. Amir thinks this will help him win the attention of girls.

B 14. What did Sohrab do to himself?

A. He tried to drown himself in the tub to commit suicide.

B. He used Amir's razor blade to try to commit suicide.

C. He used a laundry line to hang himself to try to commit suicide.

D. He electrocuted himself to try to commit suicide.

III. VOCABULARY

Answer	#	Term	Letter	Definition
T	1.	GARRULOUS	A.	Pleasantly easy to approach and to talk to; friendly; cordial; warmly polite
B	2.	FEIGNED	B.	Not real; pretended
S	3.	DEMISE	C.	A confused hand-to-hand fight or struggle among several people
F	4.	VIGIL	D.	Degree to which something is appropriate
R	5.	TENETS	E.	To find out for certain
L	6.	RETICENCE	F.	A watch kept during normal sleeping hours
G	7.	CHAGRIN	G.	A feeling of vexation, marked by disappointment or humiliation
M	8.	NONCHALANTLY	H.	Freed from guilt or blame
D	9.	APTNESS	I.	The act of employing to the greatest possible advantage
A	10.	AFFABLE	J.	Characterized by keen awareness, sharp intelligence, and often a sense of the practical
O	11.	ATONE	K.	Does a service or favor for
P	12.	OBLIVION	L.	State of being reluctant or reserved
K	13.	OBLIGES	M.	Coolly unconcerned, indifferent; casually
I	14.	EXPLOITATION	N.	Giving up; surrendering
Q	15.	EPIPHANY	O.	To make amends, as for a sin or fault
H	16.	ABSOLVE	P.	The state of being completely forgotten or unknown
J	17.	SHREWD	Q.	A sudden perception of or insight into the reality or essential meaning of something, usually initiated by some simple or commonplace occurrence or experience
E	18.	ASCERTAIN	R.	Opinions, doctrines, or principles held as being true by a person or especially by an organization
N	19.	RELINQUISHMENT	S.	Death or decline
C	20.	MELEE	T.	Excessively talkative in a rambling, roundabout manner, especially about trivial matters

UNIT RESOURCE MATERIALS

BULLETIN BOARD IDEAS *The Kite Runner*

1. Save one corner of the board for the best of students' *The Kite Runner* writing assignments.
2. Take one of the word search puzzles from the extra activities packet and with a marker copy it over in a large size on the bulletin board. Write the clue words to find to one side. Invite students prior to and after class to find the words and circle them on the bulletin board.
3. Write several of the most significant quotations from the book onto the board on brightly colored paper.
4. Make a bulletin board listing the vocabulary words for this unit. As you complete sections of the novel and discuss the vocabulary for each section, write the definitions on the bulletin board. (If your board is one students face frequently, it will help them learn the words.)
5. Create a bulletin board with photos and information about Afghanistan.
6. Create a bulletin board to promote the orphanage project your class is working on.
7. Make a bulletin board advertising other Middle Eastern authors. Include a colorful cover for each book and a short tease to get students interested.
8. Decorate your bulletin board with kites. Post articles about building kites, fighting kites, and local kite fighting tournaments.
9. Create a KWL chart for the unit on the bulletin board with your students.

RELATED TOPICS *The Kite Runner*

1. Islamic Religion
2. Afghanistan's Relationship With Surrounding Countries
3. The Immigration Process from Afghanistan to America
4. Surviving in War-Torn Countries
5. Living With Guilt
6. Atonement
7. Orphanages
8. The Adoption Process
9. Osama Bin Laden
10. Al Qaeda
11. Kite Flying, Kite Fighting, Kite Tournaments
12. Technology and Modernization in Afghanistan
13. Women's Rights in Afghanistan
14. The Taliban
15. Afghanistan's History
16. Personal Stories From Afghan People
17. The War on Terror
18. America's Relationship With Afghanistan
19. Hazara And Pashtun Conflict
20. Education in Afghanistan
21. Zahir Shah
22. Class Structure in Afghanistan
23. Successful Parent-Child Relationships

MORE ACTIVITIES *The Kite Runner*

1. Have students design a new book cover (front and back and inside flaps) for *The Kite Runner.*
2. Have students design a bulletin board (ready to be put up; not just sketched) for *The Kite Runner.*
3. Have students choose one portion of the book (with sufficient action) to rewrite in the form of a comic book. In conjunction with this assignment, have students write a composition explaining the difficulties they encountered in changing from one written form to another.
4. Have students create a soundtrack for *The Kite Runner*. Have students burn a cd of the songs, design a cd cover, and include a brief explanation as to why they selected each song.
5. Have students further explore Afghanistan's history. Have them focus on the political events and figures mentioned in the novel.
6. Have students write a short composition about a friend they had as a child and the way that relationship affected their life.
7. Amir mentions that the textbook at school leaves out information about the Hazara people being brutally murdered by the Pashtun people. Have students conduct research on other historical events left out of textbooks in various parts of the world. Ask students to reflect on how perspective affects what is put into a textbook and reflect on reasons why some places may alter their content.
8. Have students watch the films Amir loves as extra credit. Ask them to create a movie poster with a brief summary after viewing the film.
9. Have students further explore the different types of government. Ask students to research the different types of government Afghanistan has experienced throughout history and compare those with the type of government present in America.
10. Ask students to do further research on society's that have a class structure based on race or other qualities people are born with.
11. Have students create posters with information about other Middle Eastern countries. Ask them to provide information about that country and its culture.
12. Have students read the novel *Atonement* and compare it to *The Kite Runner* in more depth.
13. Have students explore patriotism in America and compare it to the patriotism other cultures have towards their home countries.
14. Amir explains that cliches are often very apt. Ask students to create a list of cliches and determine whether or not they are able to describe the situation. Ask students to try and come up with their own cliches that would work in various situations in their own lives.
15. Ask students to study religious extremists. Have them compare and contrast these extremists with other people who practice this same religion.
16. Have students research other examples of ethnic cleansing throughout history.
17. Have students find the rules to panjpar online and teach the class how to play.
18. Ask students to explore suicide attempts for people who have undergone severe trauma or unbearable situations like Sohrab did in the novel.
19. Have students explore in depth the role of Afghanistan in the September 11 terrorist attacks. Have them also explore the changes that have taken place in the country since that time.

20. Have students write a continuation to the story. Ask them to write about the lives of characters five years after the end of the story.
21. Have students create a timeline for the actions and events in each individual character's life.
22. Have students select a character from the book and complete the "I Am" poem from that character's point of view.
23. Watch the movie *The Kite Runner* by DreamWorks Entertainment and have students compare and contrast the book with the movie. (available at www.tpet.com under *The Kite Runner* title or from many other sources)
24. Let students share their creative writing stories with each other by reading them to the class.
25. In *A Separate Peace* by John Knowles, one character deals with the guilt of making his friend fall from a tree. If your students have read this book, have them compare it to The Kite Runner. If they have not read it, suggest that they read the book and make the comparison--or show the movie *A Separate Peace* (available at www.tpet.com and many other sources) and have the whole class discuss the similaities and differences between the stories.

UNIT WORD LIST *The Kite Runner*

No.	Word	Clue/Definition
1.	ALI	Servant to Baba
2.	AMIR	He returns to Afghanistan and gets Sohrab.
3.	ASSEF	The man in the Taliban with the dark sunglasses turns out to be ___________.
4.	AUTHOR	Amir's chosen career
5.	BABA	Person who arranges Amir's marriage to Soraya
6.	BASEMENT	Amir, his father, and several other people wait here while the truck is repaired to go to Pakistan.
7.	BATH	Sohrab takes a long one of these each night before he goes to bed.
8.	BEARD	Amir wears a fake ________ while traveling in Afghanistan.
9.	BIRTH	Amir's mother died while giving ____________.
10.	BIRTHDAY	Amir's father throws a huge party for Amir's ________________.
11.	BOOKS	Amir enjoys his mother's old ___________.
12.	BROTHERS	Amir and Hassan were actually half _____________.
13.	CELEBRATED	The people of Afghanistan _____________ in the streets when the Taliban took control.
14.	CEMETERY	Amir pummels Hassan with pomegranates at this place.
15.	CRY	Amir had never seen his father _______ until Ali and Hassan left.
16.	FACE	Ali's ______ and leg are both crippled/paralyzed.
17.	FARID	____ drives Amir into Afghanistan and later helps him get out safely.
18.	FIGHT	Amir has to _________ Assef until one is dead in order to earn Sohrab.
19.	FLEA	Amir and his father buy a bus so they can load it with items to sell at the ________ market.
20.	FOOD	Wahid's children wanted this, not a wristwatch.
21.	FUEL	Amir and others are placed in an empty ________ tank and transported into Pakistan.
22.	GLASS	This is on the spool of the kite to help with kite fighting.
23.	GRADUATION	Amir's father tells him he is proud of him at this ceremony.
24.	HASSAN	Amir's unfailing friend
25.	HITLER	Person Assef idolizes
26.	HOMELESS	Amir meets a __________ man who once taught with his mother.
27.	HOSPITAL	Amir works to raise money for a _________ in Afghanistan.
28.	HUT	What Hassan and his father live in
29.	JALALABAD	City where Amir and his father visit, with other family, after the tournament

No.	Word	Clue/Definition
30.	JAN	Term of endearment
31.	JUDGE	Amir's grandfather was a ________________.
32.	KAMAL	Dies on the truck ride into Pakistan
33.	KARIM	He smuggles people out of Afghanistan to safety in Pakistan.
34.	KITE	Getting the blue ___ was the most important thing to Amir.
35.	KNUCKLES	Assef is known for carrying around brass _____________.
36.	LAST	The __________ kite to fall is the most coveted by kite runners.
37.	LAWYER	Amir hires a _________ to help him with adopting Sohrab.
38.	LIP	Hassan is born with a deformity on his __________.
39.	MATTRESS	Amir hides things in this place to get Ali and Hassan fired.
40.	MINE	Ali is killed by stepping on one of these.
41.	MOSQUE	Sohrab runs way to the large ____________.
42.	MOTHER	Hassan's ______________ shows up at his home one day in need of help; Hassan and his family take her in and she becomes part of the family.
43.	ORPHANAGE	Amir's father builds this.
44.	POMEGRANATES	Fruit Amir throws at Hassan; fruit the two used to share at the top of the hill
45.	PREGNANT	Despite how hard she tried, Soraya could not get ____________.
46.	PROUD	Amir wants to make his father ___________ by winning the kite fighting tournament.
47.	RAHIM	Best friend and business partner to Amir's father
48.	RAPED	Hassan is __________ by Assef after the kite fighting tournament.
49.	RAZOR	Sohrab uses this to attempt suicide.
50.	READ	What Amir and Hassan do at the top of the hill
51.	RUNNER	A kite ___ tries to catch a falling kite before it lands.
52.	RUSSIA	Soldiers from this country are in Afghanistan; they are the reason many people are fleeing.
53.	SERVANTS	Amir asks his father if he would ever get new ______________.
54.	SHEEP	Amir compares both Hassan and Sohrab's eyes to the eyes of this animal.
55.	SILENT	Sohrab is __________ when he gets to America.
56.	SING	Soraya's mother is never allowed to do this in public.
57.	SINGERS	Hassan's mother ran off with a clan of ________ and dancers after giving birth.
58.	SLINGSHOT	Weapon used by both Hassan and Sohrab to save Amir
59.	SMILE	Sohrab does this at the Afghan New Year's Celebration.
60.	SOCCER	Amir watches two people get stoned to death at a ______ game.
61.	SOHRAB	Hassan's son
62.	SORAYA	Amir's wife

No.	Word	Clue/Definition
63.	STAMPS	Amir's father is insulted that Americans gave him food __________.
64.	STORY	Amir gets caught giving Soraya one of these.
65.	STREET	Place where Hassan was shot and killed
66.	SURGERY	Amir's father gives Hassan this gift for his birthday.
67.	TAHERI	Soraya's father: General ___
68.	TALIBAN	Violent leaders of Afghanistan
69.	TEACHER	Soraya's chosen profession
70.	THEFT	Amir's father believes ____ is the root of all other sins.
71.	TREASON	Amir is told he could be arrested for _________ since he abandoned the country and went to live in America.
72.	TWELVE	At the age of ____ Amir's life changed and he became who he is today.
73.	UNCLE	Soraya's ________ is able to help get Sohrab into America.
74.	WINTER	Favorite seasons for kids in Kabul; kite fighting season

CROSSWORD - The Kite Runner

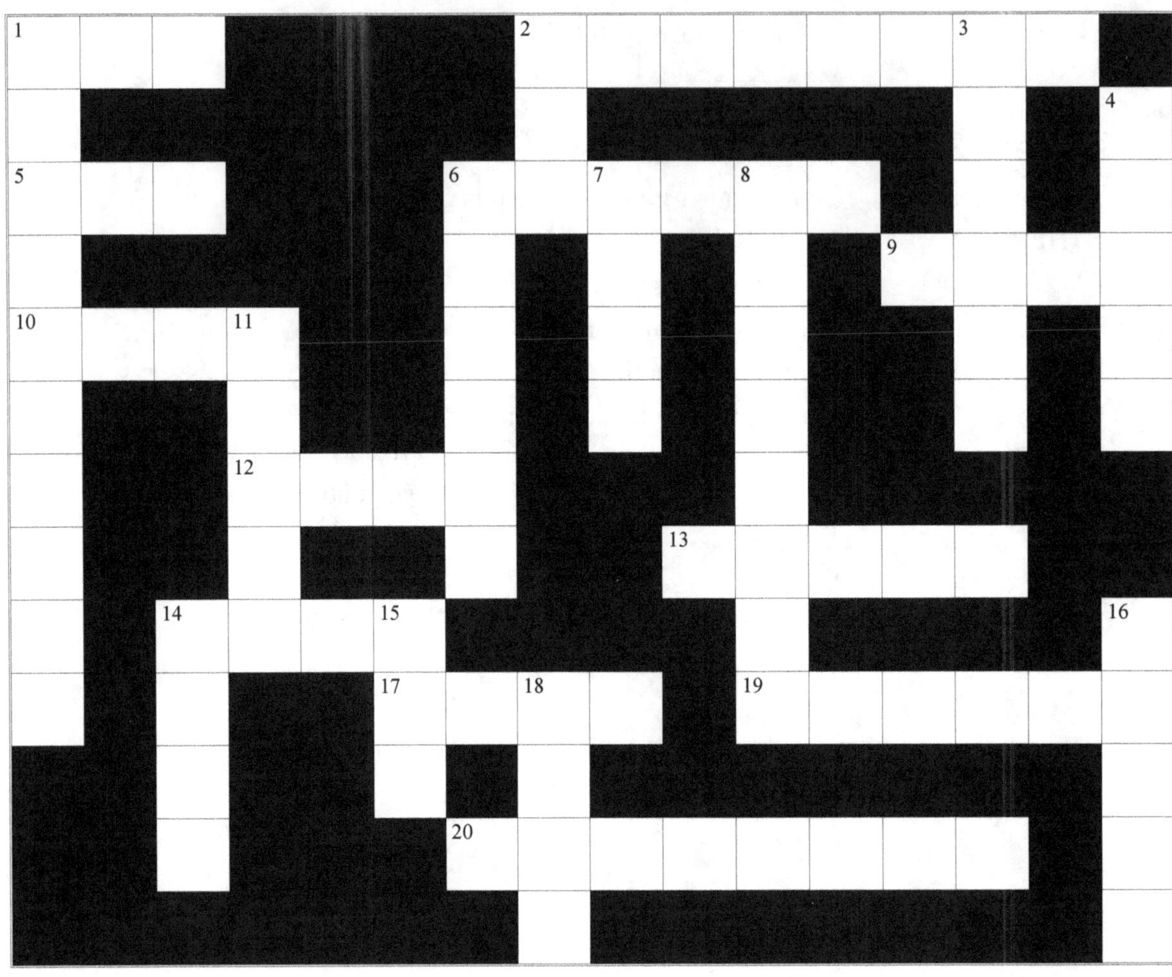

Across

1. Amir had never seen his father _______ until Ali and Hassan left.
2. Amir meets a __________ man who once taught with his mother.
5. Hassan is born with a deformity on his __________.
6. Amir's father is insulted that Americans gave him food__________.
9. What Amir and Hassan do at the top of the hill
10. Amir enjoys his mother's old ___________.
12. Ali is killed by stepping on one of these.
13. Sohrab uses this to attempt suicide.
14. Amir and his father buy a bus so they can load it with items to sell at the ________ market.
17. The __________ kite to fall is the most coveted by kite runners.
19. At the age of ____ Amir's life changed and he became who he is today.
20. Assef is known for carrying around brass _____________.

Down

1. The people of Afghanistan _____________ in the streets when the Taliban took control.
2. What Hassan and his father live in
3. Place where Hassan was shot and killed
4. Amir's grandfather was a ________________.
6. Amir watches two people get stoned to death at a _______ game.
7. He returns to Afghanistan and gets Sohrab.
8. Despite how hard she tried, Soraya could not get ____________.
11. Dies on the truck ride into Pakistan
14. Amir and others are placed in an empty ________ tank and transported into Pakistan.
15. Best friend and business partner to Amir's father
16. Amir wears a fake ________ while traveling in Afghanistan.
18. Soraya's mother is never allowed to do this in public.

CROSSWORD ANSWER KEY - The Kite Runner

1 C	R	Y					2 H	O	M	E	L	E	3 S	S	
E							U						T		4 J
5 L	I	P				6 S	T	7 A	M	8 P	S		R		U
E						O		M		R		9 R	E	A	D
10 B	O	O	11 K			C		I		E			E		G
R			A			C		R		G			T		E
A			12 M	I	N	E				N					
T			A			R			13 R	A	Z	O	R		
E		14 F	L	E	15 A					N					16 B
D		U			17 L	A	18 S	T		19 T	W	E	L	V	E
		E			I		I								A
		L				20 K	N	U	C	K	L	E	S		R
							G								D

Across

1. Amir had never seen his father _______ until Ali and Hassan left.
2. Amir meets a __________ man who once taught with his mother.
5. Hassan is born with a deformity on his __________.
6. Amir's father is insulted that Americans gave him food__________.
9. What Amir and Hassan do at the top of the hill
10. Amir enjoys his mother's old ___________.
12. Ali is killed by stepping on one of these.
13. Sohrab uses this to attempt suicide.
14. Amir and his father buy a bus so they can load it with items to sell at the ________ market.
17. The __________ kite to fall is the most coveted by kite runners.
19. At the age of____ Amir's life changed and he became who he is today.
20. Assef is known for carrying around brass _____________.

Down

1. The people of Afghanistan _____________ in the streets when the Taliban took control.
2. What Hassan and his father live in
3. Place where Hassan was shot and killed
4. Amir's grandfather was a ________________.
6. Amir watches two people get stoned to death at a _______ game.
7. He returns to Afghanistan and gets Sohrab.
8. Despite how hard she tried, Soraya could not get ____________.
11. Dies on the truck ride into Pakistan
14. Amir and others are placed in an empty ________ tank and transported into Pakistan.
15. Best friend and business partner to Amir's father
16. Amir wears a fake ________ while traveling in Afghanistan.
18. Soraya's mother is never allowed to do this in public.

WORD SEARCH - The Kite Runner

B	I	R	T	H	F	T	S	S	E	R	T	T	A	M	Q	L	B	H	K
I	Y	Y	U	P	H	N	S	R	U	H	U	K	W	Q	T	I	E	A	F
R	Q	T	V	G	F	E	K	E	T	R	E	N	N	E	C	P	A	S	H
T	G	N	I	S	L	L	A	H	A	S	G	T	N	U	L	L	R	S	B
H	A	F	W	E	E	I	R	T	H	H	D	E	G	E	C	V	D	A	P
D	U	M	M	J	A	S	I	O	E	E	U	E	R	Y	R	K	E	N	C
A	T	O	O	N	A	K	M	R	R	E	J	R	G	Y	S	K	L	S	T
Y	H	J	F	S	C	L	T	B	I	P	T	T	C	S	O	G	P	E	H
Y	O	Q	J	J	Q	N	A	K	L	A	P	S	A	R	R	M	D	F	S
Y	R	O	T	S	A	U	D	L	L	G	D	L	T	E	A	C	H	E	R
F	P	F	G	N	V	H	E	I	A	E	G	S	S	T	Y	H	F	Y	C
F	Y	J	G	R	W	M	B	N	T	B	L	F	S	G	A	H	A	R	T
P	J	E	D	K	I	A	O	A	F	X	A	D	C	S	I	D	R	E	X
F	R	C	D	A	N	F	R	T	C	N	W	D	M	T	M	K	I	T	V
P	P	O	K	M	T	B	F	L	H	N	Y	B	L	P	B	I	D	E	T
Q	O	L	A	A	E	W	K	A	O	E	E	E	O	R	Z	T	L	M	T
F	F	U	E	L	R	U	S	S	I	A	R	A	Z	O	R	E	M	E	K
R	Q	N	E	I	I	S	A	I	O	W	G	C	N	U	K	I	L	C	M
X	I	C	M	D	E	E	T	N	H	H	D	R	L	D	H	C	B	A	M
M	W	A	E	F	R	M	H	G	L	A	R	Y	J	A	N	B	A	F	F
N	Q	P	V	T	S	P	E	E	E	A	Q	A	R	U	J	A	B	V	Z
F	A	R	M	Q	B	L	F	R	M	H	S	G	B	S	X	T	A	Q	D
R	S	E	R	V	A	N	T	S	K	T	R	T	V	Z	M	H	S	Z	P

ALI	FACE	KAMAL	RAPED	STORY
AMIR	FARID	KARIM	RAZOR	STREET
ASSEF	FIGHT	KITE	READ	SURGERY
AUTHOR	FLEA	KNUCKLES	RUNNER	TAHERI
BABA	FOOD	LAST	RUSSIA	TALIBAN
BATH	FUEL	LAWYER	SERVANTS	TEACHER
BEARD	GLASS	LIP	SHEEP	THEFT
BIRTH	HASSAN	MATTRESS	SILENT	TREASON
BIRTHDAY	HITLER	MINE	SING	TWELVE
BOOK	HOMELESS	MOSQUE	SINGERS	UNCLE
BROTHERS	HUT	MOTHER	SMILE	WINTER
CELEBRATED	JALALABAD	PREGNANT	SOHRAB	
CEMETERY	JAN	PROUD	SORAYA	
CRY	JUDGE	RAHIM	STAMPS	

WORD SEARCH ANSWER KEY - The Kite Runner

B	I	R	T	H		T	S	S	E	R	T	T	A	M		L	B	H	
I			U		H	N	S	R	U		U	K	W			I	E	A	
R		T		G	F	E	K	E	T	R	E	N	N	E		P	A	S	
T	G	N	I	S	L	L	A	H	A	S	G	T	N	U	L		R	S	
H	A	F		E	E	I	R	T	H	H	D	E		E	C	V	D	A	
D	U	M	M	J	A	S	I	O	E	E	U	E	R		R	K	E	N	
A	T	O	O		A		M	R	R	E	J	R		Y	S		L	S	
Y	H			S		L	T	B	I	P	T	T		S	O		P	E	
	O				Q	N	A			A		S	A		R	M			S
Y	R	O	T	S	A	U		L	L		D	L	T	E	A	C	H	E	R
				N			E	I	A	E	G			T	Y		F	Y	
			G		W	M	B		T	B	L		S		A	H	A	R	
		E		K	I	A	O	A			A			S	I		R	E	
	R		D	A	N		R	T			W	D		T	M	K	I	T	
P		O		M	T	B			H	N	Y	B	L	P		I	D	E	
	O		A	A	E			A	O	E	E	E	O	R		T	L	M	
F	F	U	E	L	R	U	S	S	I	A	R	A	Z	O	R	E	M	E	
		N	E	I	I	S	A	I	O			C		U	K	I	L	C	
	I	C	M	D	E	E	T	N		H	D	R		D	H	C	B	A	
M		A	E	F	R		H	G	L	A	R	Y	J	A	N	B	A	F	
		P		T			E	E	E	A		A	R	U		A	B		
	A						F	R			S		B			T	A		
R	S	E	R	V	A	N	T	S				T				H			

ALI	FACE	KAMAL	RAPED	STORY
AMIR	FARID	KARIM	RAZOR	STREET
ASSEF	FIGHT	KITE	READ	SURGERY
AUTHOR	FLEA	KNUCKLES	RUNNER	TAHERI
BABA	FOOD	LAST	RUSSIA	TALIBAN
BATH	FUEL	LAWYER	SERVANTS	TEACHER
BEARD	GLASS	LIP	SHEEP	THEFT
BIRTH	HASSAN	MATTRESS	SILENT	TREASON
BIRTHDAY	HITLER	MINE	SING	TWELVE
BOOK	HOMELESS	MOSQUE	SINGERS	UNCLE
BROTHERS	HUT	MOTHER	SMILE	WINTER
CELEBRATED	JALALABAD	PREGNANT	SOHRAB	
CEMETERY	JAN	PROUD	SORAYA	
CRY	JUDGE	RAHIM	STAMPS	

MATCHING 1 *The Kite Runner*

____ 1.	TAHERI	A.	City where Amir and his father visit, with other family, after the tournament
____ 2.	BIRTHDAY	B.	He returns to Afghanistan and gets Sohrab.
____ 3.	KAMAL	C.	Amir's chosen career
____ 4.	GRADUATION	D.	Servant to Baba
____ 5.	SORAYA	E.	Best friend and business partner to Amir's father
____ 6.	BABA	F.	Amir hires a _________ to help him with adopting Sohrab.
____ 7.	TALIBAN	G.	Soraya's chosen profession
____ 8.	SOHRAB	H.	Person who arranges Amir's marriage to Soraya
____ 9.	FARID	I.	He smuggles people out of Afghanistan to safety in Pakistan.
____ 10.	JALALABAD	J.	Person Assef idolizes
____ 11.	RAHIM	K.	Hassan's son
____ 12.	ALI	L.	Soraya's father: General ___
____ 13.	HASSAN	M.	Amir's wife
____ 14.	AMIR	N.	Amir's father throws a huge party for Amir's ________________.
____ 15.	ASSEF	O.	Amir's unfailing friend
____ 16.	AUTHOR	P.	The man in the Taliban with the dark sunglasses turns out to be ___________.
____ 17.	TEACHER	Q.	____ drives Amir into Afghanistan and later helps him get out safely.
____ 18.	KARIM	R.	Amir's father tells him he is proud of him at this ceremony.
____ 19.	HITLER	S.	Dies on the truck ride into Pakistan
____ 20.	LAWYER	T.	Violent leaders of Afghanistan

MATCHING 1 ANSWER KEY *The Kite Runner*

L	1. TAHERI	A. City where Amir and his father visit, with other family, after the tournament
N	2. BIRTHDAY	B. He returns to Afghanistan and gets Sohrab.
S	3. KAMAL	C. Amir's chosen career
R	4. GRADUATION	D. Servant to Baba
M	5. SORAYA	E. Best friend and business partner to Amir's father
H	6. BABA	F. Amir hires a _________ to help him with adopting Sohrab.
T	7. TALIBAN	G. Soraya's chosen profession
K	8. SOHRAB	H. Person who arranges Amir's marriage to Soraya
Q	9. FARID	I. He smuggles people out of Afghanistan to safety in Pakistan.
A	10. JALALABAD	J. Person Assef idolizes
E	11. RAHIM	K. Hassan's son
D	12. ALI	L. Soraya's father: General ___
O	13. HASSAN	M. Amir's wife
B	14. AMIR	N. Amir's father throws a huge party for Amir's ________________.
P	15. ASSEF	O. Amir's unfailing friend
C	16. AUTHOR	P. The man in the Taliban with the dark sunglasses turns out to be ___________.
G	17. TEACHER	Q. ____ drives Amir into Afghanistan and later helps him get out safely.
I	18. KARIM	R. Amir's father tells him he is proud of him at this ceremony.
J	19. HITLER	S. Dies on the truck ride into Pakistan
F	20. LAWYER	T. Violent leaders of Afghanistan

MATCHING 2 *The Kite Runner*

____ 1.	SMILE	A.	Amir's father builds this.
____ 2.	JAN	B.	Person who arranges Amir's marriage to Soraya
____ 3.	ALI	C.	____ drives Amir into Afghanistan and later helps him get out safely.
____ 4.	HASSAN	D.	Sohrab runs way to the large ____________.
____ 5.	AMIR	E.	He returns to Afghanistan and gets Sohrab.
____ 6.	HOSPITAL	F.	Sohrab does this at the Afghan New Year's Celebration.
____ 7.	ASSEF	G.	Hassan's son
____ 8.	KARIM	H.	Amir's unfailing friend
____ 9.	HITLER	I.	He smuggles people out of Afghanistan to safety in Pakistan.
____ 10.	FOOD	J.	The man in the Taliban with the dark sunglasses turns out to be ___________.
____ 11.	ORPHANAGE	K.	Soraya's mother is never allowed to do this in public.
____ 12.	MOSQUE	L.	Amir's grandfather was a ________________.
____ 13.	FARID	M.	Person Assef idolizes
____ 14.	SOHRAB	N.	Amir works to raise money for a _________ in Afghanistan.
____ 15.	TALIBAN	O.	Servant to Baba
____ 16.	SING	P.	Term of endearment
____ 17.	BABA	Q.	Amir gets caught giving Soraya one of these.
____ 18.	STORY	R.	Wahid's children wanted this, not a wristwatch.
____ 19.	JUDGE	S.	Best friend and business partner to Amir's father
____ 20.	RAHIM	T.	Violent leaders of Afghanistan

MATCHING 2 ANSWER KEY *The Kite Runner*

F	1. SMILE	A. Amir's father builds this.
P	2. JAN	B. Person who arranges Amir's marriage to Soraya
O	3. ALI	C. ____ drives Amir into Afghanistan and later helps him get out safely.
H	4. HASSAN	D. Sohrab runs way to the large ___________.
E	5. AMIR	E. He returns to Afghanistan and gets Sohrab.
N	6. HOSPITAL	F. Sohrab does this at the Afghan New Year's Celebration.
J	7. ASSEF	G. Hassan's son
I	8. KARIM	H. Amir's unfailing friend
M	9. HITLER	I. He smuggles people out of Afghanistan to safety in Pakistan.
R	10. FOOD	J. The man in the Taliban with the dark sunglasses turns out to be __________.
A	11. ORPHANAGE	K. Soraya's mother is never allowed to do this in public.
D	12. MOSQUE	L. Amir's grandfather was a _______________.
C	13. FARID	M. Person Assef idolizes
G	14. SOHRAB	N. Amir works to raise money for a _________ in Afghanistan.
T	15. TALIBAN	O. Servant to Baba
K	16. SING	P. Term of endearment
B	17. BABA	Q. Amir gets caught giving Soraya one of these.
Q	18. STORY	R. Wahid's children wanted this, not a wristwatch.
L	19. JUDGE	S. Best friend and business partner to Amir's father
S	20. RAHIM	T. Violent leaders of Afghanistan

JUGGLE LETTERS 1 *The Kite Runner*

_______________ = 1. ARZOR
Sohrab uses this to attempt suicide.

_______________ = 2. REPDA
Hassan is __________ by Assef after the kite fighting tournament.

_______________ = 3. TINREW
Favorite seasons for kids in Kabul; kite fighting season

_______________ = 4. TREMCEEY
Amir pummels Hassan with pomegranates at this place.

_______________ = 5. TOLHPSIA
Amir works to raise money for a _________ in Afghanistan.

_______________ = 6. AERGTNNP
Despite how hard she tried, Soraya could not get ____________.

_______________ = 7. SAGSL
This is on the spool of the kite to help with kite fighting.

_______________ = 8. OGSILSHNT
Weapon used by both Hassan and Sohrab to save Amir

_______________ = 9. KLSCNUKE
Assef is known for carrying around brass _____________.

_______________ = 10. AVSRTSNE
Amir asks his father if he would ever get new ______________.

_______________ = 11. BLAAJAADL
City where Amir and his father visit, with other family, after the tournament

_______________ = 12. MSOEUQ
Sohrab runs way to the large ____________.

_______________ = 13. ARDEB
Amir wears a fake ________ while traveling in Afghanistan.

_______________ = 14. SHETORRB
Amir and Hassan were actually half _____________.

_______________ = 15. DECETRBALE
The people of Afghanistan _____________ in the streets when the Taliban took control.

_______________ = 16. AYROAS
Amir's wife

_______________ = 17. ASSMTP
Amir's father is insulted that Americans gave him food __________.

_______________ = 18. TMASRTES
Amir hides things in this place to get Ali and Hassan fired.

_______________ = 19. RTMEANOAGPES
Fruit Amir throws at Hassan; fruit the two used to share at the top of the hill

_______________ = 20. TEHTF
Amir's father believes ____ is the root of all other sins.

JUGGLE LETTERS 1 ANSWER KEY *The Kite Runner*

RAZOR = 1. ARZOR
Sohrab uses this to attempt suicide.

RAPED = 2. REPDA
Hassan is __________ by Assef after the kite fighting tournament.

WINTER = 3. TINREW
Favorite seasons for kids in Kabul; kite fighting season

CEMETERY = 4. TREMCEEY
Amir pummels Hassan with pomegranates at this place.

HOSPITAL = 5. TOLHPSIA
Amir works to raise money for a _________ in Afghanistan.

PREGNANT = 6. AERGTNNP
Despite how hard she tried, Soraya could not get ____________.

GLASS = 7. SAGSL
This is on the spool of the kite to help with kite fighting.

SLINGSHOT = 8. OGSILSHNT
Weapon used by both Hassan and Sohrab to save Amir

KNUCKLES = 9. KLSCNUKE
Assef is known for carrying around brass _____________.

SERVANTS = 10. AVSRTSNE
Amir asks his father if he would ever get new ______________.

JALALABAD = 11. BLAAJAADL
City where Amir and his father visit, with other family, after the tournament

MOSQUE = 12. MSOEUQ
Sohrab runs way to the large ____________.

BEARD = 13. ARDEB
Amir wears a fake ________ while traveling in Afghanistan.

BROTHERS = 14. SHETORRB
Amir and Hassan were actually half _____________.

CELEBRATED = 15. DECETRBALE
The people of Afghanistan _____________ in the streets when the Taliban took control.

SORAYA = 16. AYROAS
Amir's wife

STAMPS = 17. ASSMTP
Amir's father is insulted that Americans gave him food __________.

MATTRESS = 18. TMASRTES
Amir hides things in this place to get Ali and Hassan fired.

POMEGRANATES = 19. RTMEANOAGPES
Fruit Amir throws at Hassan; fruit the two used to share at the top of the hill

THEFT = 20. TEHTF
Amir's father believes ____ is the root of all other sins.

JUGGLE LETTERS 2 *The Kite Runner*

_______________ = 1. HMAIR
Best friend and business partner to Amir's father

_______________ = 2. NIRWET
Favorite seasons for kids in Kabul; kite fighting season

_______________ = 3. ERAD
What Amir and Hassan do at the top of the hill

_______________ = 4. RUASSI
Soldiers from this country are in Afghanistan; they are the reason many people are fleeing.

_______________ = 5. ORASAY
Amir's wife

_______________ = 6. ATALBIN
Violent leaders of Afghanistan

_______________ = 7. BSRAOH
Hassan's son

_______________ = 8. HOEMESLS
Amir meets a __________ man who once taught with his mother.

_______________ = 9. TEARNOS
Amir is told he could be arrested for __________ since he abandoned the country and went to live in America.

_______________ = 10. GDJEU
Amir's grandfather was a ________________.

_______________ = 11. OKBSO
Amir enjoys his mother's old ___________.

_______________ = 12. CAEF
Ali's ______ and leg are both crippled/paralyzed.

_______________ = 13. PIL
Hassan is born with a deformity on his __________.

_______________ = 14. KIMAR
He smuggles people out of Afghanistan to safety in Pakistan.

_______________ = 15. MEIN
Ali is killed by stepping on one of these.

_______________ = 16. TESETR
Place where Hassan was shot and killed

_______________ = 17. LUCNE
Soraya's ________ is able to help get Sohrab into America.

_______________ = 18. NERNUR
A kite ___ tries to catch a falling kite before it lands.

_______________ = 19. EMYCRETE
Amir pummels Hassan with pomegranates at this place.

_______________ = 20. SNEILT
Sohrab is __________ when he gets to America.

JUGGLE LETTERS 2 ANSWER KEY *The Kite Runner*

RAHIM = 1. HMAIR
Best friend and business partner to Amir's father

WINTER = 2. NIRWET
Favorite seasons for kids in Kabul; kite fighting season

READ = 3. ERAD
What Amir and Hassan do at the top of the hill

RUSSIA = 4. RUASSI
Soldiers from this country are in Afghanistan; they are the reason many people are fleeing.

SORAYA = 5. ORASAY
Amir's wife

TALIBAN = 6. ATALBIN
Violent leaders of Afghanistan

SOHRAB = 7. BSRAOH
Hassan's son

HOMELESS = 8. HOEMESLS
Amir meets a __________ man who once taught with his mother.

TREASON = 9. TEARNOS
Amir is told he could be arrested for __________ since he abandoned the country and went to live in America.

JUDGE = 10. GDJEU
Amir's grandfather was a ________________.

BOOKS = 11. OKBSO
Amir enjoys his mother's old ___________.

FACE = 12. CAEF
Ali's ______ and leg are both crippled/paralyzed.

LIP = 13. PIL
Hassan is born with a deformity on his __________.

KARIM = 14. KIMAR
He smuggles people out of Afghanistan to safety in Pakistan.

MINE = 15. MEIN
Ali is killed by stepping on one of these.

STREET = 16. TESETR
Place where Hassan was shot and killed

UNCLE = 17. LUCNE
Soraya's ________ is able to help get Sohrab into America.

RUNNER = 18. NERNUR
A kite ___ tries to catch a falling kite before it lands.

CEMETERY = 19. EMYCRETE
Amir pummels Hassan with pomegranates at this place.

SILENT = 20. SNEILT
Sohrab is __________ when he gets to America.

VOCABULARY RESOURCE MATERIALS

The Kite Runner Vocabulary

No.	Word	Clue/Definition
1.	ABSOLVE	Freed from guilt or blame
2.	ADVERSARY	Opponent; enemy
3.	AFFABLE	Pleasantly easy to approach and to talk to; friendly; cordial; warmly polite
4.	AFFLUENT	Generously supplied with money, property, or possessions; prosperous or rich
5.	ALLEVIATED	Made easier to endure; lessened
6.	AMBIVALENT	Uncertain or unable to decide about what course to follow
7.	AMBLED	Moved with a slow, easy walk; strolled
8.	ANONYMITY	The quality or state of being unknown or unacknowledged
9.	APPREHENSIVELY	Showing unease or fearfulness about something that might happen
10.	APTNESS	Degree to which something is appropriate
11.	ARDUOUS	Requiring great exertion; laborious; difficult
12.	ARID	Being without moisture; extremely dry; parched
13.	ARRAY	An impressively large number
14.	ASCERTAIN	To find out for certain
15.	ATONE	To make amends, as for a sin or fault
16.	ATROPHIED	Wasted; withered; shriveled
17.	AUSTERE	Grave; strict; solemn; serious
18.	AVERTING	Preventing something from occurring
19.	BENEVOLENCE	An inclination to perform kind, charitable acts
20.	BLUDGEONED	Hit or overcame
21.	CHAGRIN	A feeling of vexation, marked by disappointment or humiliation
22.	CHASM	A pronounced difference of opinion, interests, or loyalty
23.	CONJURE	To call or bring into existence by or as if by magic
24.	CONTEMPTUOUS	Showing or expressing contempt or disdain; scornful
25.	COY	Affectedly modest or shy especially in a playful or provocative way
26.	DAUNTING	Discouraging through fear
27.	DEMISE	Death or decline
28.	DISMAY	Agitation; perturbation; alarm
29.	DIVERT	To distract from serious occupation; entertain or amuse
30.	ECCENTRIC	Departing from a recognized, conventional, or established norm
31.	EMBODIMENT	To exemplify in concrete form
32.	EMPATHY	Understanding of another's situation, feelings, and motives
33.	EPIPHANY	A sudden perception of or insight into the reality or essential meaning of something, usually initiated by some simple or commonplace occurrence or experience

No.	Word	Clue/Definition
34.	ERRONEOUS	Containing error; mistaken; incorrect; wrong
35.	EXASPERATED	Made very angry or impatient; annoyed greatly
36.	EXPLOITATION	The act of employing to the greatest possible advantage
37.	EXUDED	To project or display; radiate
38.	FACADE	An artificial or deceptive front
39.	FEIGNED	Not real; pretended
40.	FURTIVE	Secret; sly; shifty
41.	FUTILITY	Characterized by having no useful result; uselessness
42.	GARRULOUS	Excessively talkative in a rambling, roundabout manner, especially about trivial matters
43.	GRIMACE	A facial expression that indicates disapproval or pain
44.	GUILELESS	Sincere; honest; straightforward
45.	HAPHAZARDLY	In a random manner; without care
46.	IMMINENT	Likely to occur at any moment; impending
47.	IMPASSIVE	Without emotion; unmoved
48.	IMPUNITY	Exemption from punishment, penalty, or harm
49.	INCESSANT	Continuing without interruption; ceaseless; unending
50.	INDIGNATION	Anger aroused by something unjust, mean, or unworthy
51.	INSINUATION	An indirect or covert suggestion or hint especially of a derogatory nature
52.	IRREVOCABLY	Not to be revoked or recalled; unable to be repealed or annulled; unalterable
53.	LEER	To look with a sidelong glance, especially with sexual desire or sly and malicious intent
54.	LUCRATIVE	Profitable; moneymaking
55.	LUNACY	Great or wild foolishness; insanity
56.	MELEE	A confused hand-to-hand fight or struggle among several people
57.	METICULOUS	Extremely careful and precise; paying great attention to details
58.	MILIEU	An environment or a setting; surroundings
59.	MOROSE	Melancholy; gloomy
60.	NEGATE	To make ineffective or invalid; nullify
61.	NONCHALANTLY	Coolly unconcerned, indifferent; casually
62.	NOTORIOUSLY	Known widely and usually unfavorably known
63.	NOVELTY	Something unique or new
64.	NUANCES	Subtle differences or distinctions in expression, meaning, or response
65.	OBLIGES	Does a service or favor for
66.	OBLIVION	The state of being completely forgotten or unknown
67.	PALLIATIVE	Relieving or soothing the symptoms of a disease or disorder without affecting a cure
68.	PERIPHERY	The edge or outskirts

No.	Word	Clue/Definition
69.	PILGRIMAGE	A journey, especially a long one, made to some sacred place as an act of religious devotion
70.	PRAGMATIC	Dealing or concerned with facts or actual occurrences; practical
71.	PRECIPITOUS	Extremely steep
72.	PROGNOSIS	A prediction of the probable course and outcome of a disease
73.	PROTOCOL	A code of correct conduct
74.	PRUDENCE	Caution with regard to practical matters; regard for one's own interests
75.	QUELLED	Pacified: quieted or suppressed
76.	QUERIES	Questions; inquiries
77.	QUEUE	A file or line, especially of people waiting in turn
78.	REDEMPTION	To make up for; make amends for
79.	RELINQUISHMENT	Giving up; surrendering
80.	REMORSE	Deep and painful regret for wrongdoing
81.	RETICENCE	State of being reluctant or reserved
82.	REVERIES	Daydreams
83.	ROTUND	Round in shape; plump; fat
84.	RUEFUL	Causing sorrow or pity; deplorable; mournful
85.	SHEEN	Glistening brightness; radiance
86.	SHREWD	Characterized by keen awareness, sharp intelligence, and often a sense of the practical
87.	SQUALID	Foul and repulsive, as from lack of care or cleanliness; neglected and filthy
88.	SURLY	Rude or bad-tempered; unfriendly or hostile
89.	SURREAL	Having the disorienting, hallucinatory quality of a dream; seeming unreal; fantastic
90.	TEEMING	Abounding or swarming with something, as with people
91.	TENETS	Opinions, doctrines, or principles held as being true by a person or especially by an organization
92.	TERSE	Brief and to the point
93.	TREPIDATION	A state of alarm or dread; apprehension
94.	UNABASHEDLY	Not concealed or disguised; obviously
95.	UNREQUITED	Not returned or reciprocated
96.	UNSCRUPULOUS	Having no conscience or principles; oblivious to what is right or honorable
97.	UNWITTING	Unintentional; accidental; not knowing; unaware
98.	VALIANT	Boldly courageous; brave
99.	VIGIL	A watch kept during normal sleeping hours

VOCABULARY CROSSWORD - The Kite Runner

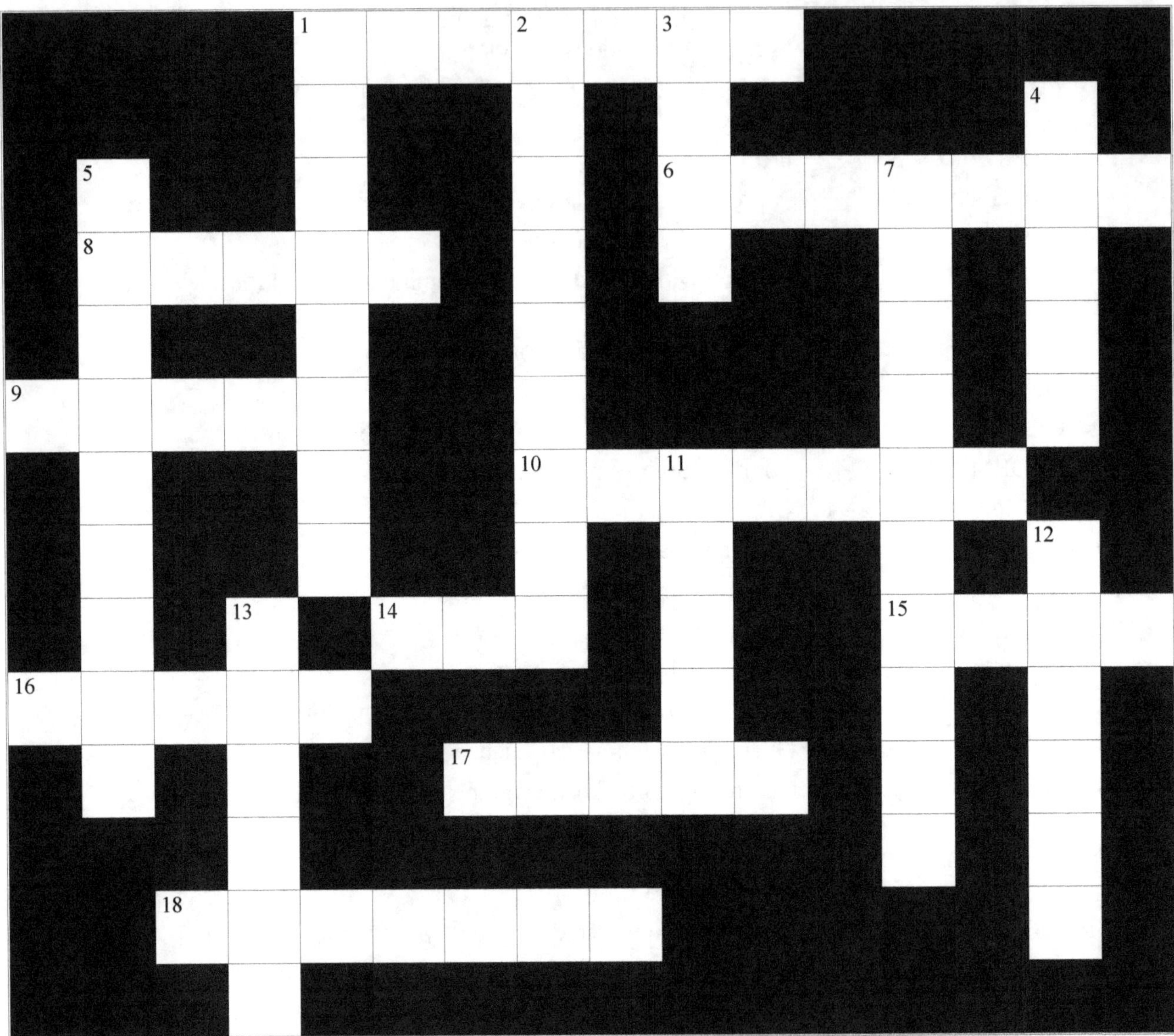

Across

1. Pleasantly easy to approach and to talk to; friendly; cordial: warmly polite
6. Understanding of another's situation, feelings, and motives
8. Rude or bad-tempered; unfriendly or hostile
9. A confused hand-to-hand fight or struggle among several people
10. Freed from guilt or blame
14. Affectedly modest or shy especially in a playful or provocative way
15. Being without moisture; extremely dry; parched
16. A watch kept during normal sleeping hours
17. To make amends, as for a sin or fault
18. Requiring great exertion; laborious; difficult

Down

1. Generously supplied with money, property, or possessions; prosperous or rich
2. Opponent; enemy
3. To look with a sidelong glance, especially with sexual desire or sly and malicious intent
4. A pronounced difference of opinion, interests, or loyalty
5. To find out for certain
7. Made easier to endure; lessened
11. Glistening brightness; radiance
12. Agitation; perturbation; alarm
13. To distract from serious occupation; entertain or amuse

VOCABULARY CROSSWORD ANSWER KEY - The Kite Runner

				1 A	F	F	2 A	B	3 L	E					
				F			D		E					4 C	
	5 A			F			V		6 E	M	P	7 A	T	H	Y
	8 S	U	R	L	Y		E		R			L		A	
	C			U			R					L		S	
9 M	E	L	E	E			S					E		M	
	R			N			10 A	B	11 S	O	L	V	E		
	T			T			R		H			I		12 D	
	A		13 D		14 C	O	Y		E			15 A	R	I	D
16 V	I	G	I	L					E			T		S	
	N		V			17 A	T	O	N	E		E		M	
			E									D		A	
		18 A	R	D	U	O	U	S						Y	
			T												

Across

1. Pleasantly easy to approach and to talk to; friendly; cordial: warmly polite
6. Understanding of another's situation, feelings, and motives
8. Rude or bad-tempered; unfriendly or hostile
9. A confused hand-to-hand fight or struggle among several people
10. Freed from guilt or blame
14. Affectedly modest or shy especially in a playful or provocative way
15. Being without moisture; extremely dry; parched
16. A watch kept during normal sleeping hours
17. To make amends, as for a sin or fault
18. Requiring great exertion; laborious; difficult

Down

1. Generously supplied with money, property, or possessions; prosperous or rich
2. Opponent; enemy
3. To look with a sidelong glance, especially with sexual desire or sly and malicious intent
4. A pronounced difference of opinion, interests, or loyalty
5. To find out for certain
7. Made easier to endure; lessened
11. Glistening brightness; radiance
12. Agitation; perturbation; alarm
13. To distract from serious occupation; entertain or amuse

VOCABULARY WORD SEARCH - The Kite Runner

A T O N E Y L E V I S N E H E R P P A H
P M N F V Q N P D T A F I K V R A Q N K
R J C G I B M I R P W E M S F E L F S T
A G V Q T K L Z T X Q I P E F G L P L N
G H Y Z R A V N T M D G A C L A I P E Q
M C A K U M E L I E N N S N A M A T V X
A H M Q F S O L H R U E S A E I T E I G
T A S E S H I R G E T D I U R R I R T B
I S I X L E Z F O T O T V N R G V S A Y
C M D Q U E R I E S R U E F U L E E R H
H B Y J U N E L E U E S X N S I Y M C Z
A N T E B D B G N A I I P C E P Y P U K
G Q U J E A I I S M N S L O M T L A L X
R Q D L F L A U E K E O O Y E N S T U H
I B B F B T O D I T G N I O T E A H N C
N M A O R U Y A R R A G T B I N F Y W S
A N C E D M E E E F T O A L C I F T I W
L V C R V V V R V Z E R T I U M L I T S
Q S A D L I W S E F S P I V L M U N T L
A L I O D D G W R Z D D O I O I E U I P
J R S E C A M I R G J W N O U H N P N B
A B R C M Q U E L L E D K N S J T M G L
A L L E V I A T E D W E R H S S N I N Z

ABSOLVE
AFFABLE
AFFLUENT
ALLEVIATED
AMBLED
APPREHENSIVELY
APTNESS
ARDUOUS
ARID
ARRAY
ASCERTAIN
ATONE
AUSTERE
CHAGRIN

CHASM
COY
DEMISE
DISMAY
DIVERT
EMPATHY
EXPLOITATION
FEIGNED
FURTIVE
GRIMACE
IMMINENT
IMPASSIVE
IMPUNITY
LEER

LUCRATIVE
MELEE
METICULOUS
MILIEU
MOROSE
NEGATE
NUANCES
OBLIGES
OBLIVION
PALLIATIVE
PILGRIMAGE
PRAGMATIC
PROGNOSIS
QUELLED

QUERIES
QUEUE
REVERIES
ROTUND
RUEFUL
SHEEN
SHREWD
SQUALID
SURLY
SURREAL
TENETS
TERSE
UNWITTING
VIGIL

VOCABULARY WORD SEARCH ANSWER KEY - The Kite Runner

A	T	O	N	E	Y	L	E	V	I	S	N	E	H	E	R	P	P	A
P				V				D		A	F	I				A		
R				I			I		P		E	M	S		E	L		
A				T		L		T			I	P	E		G	L		
G		Y		R	A		N		M	D	G	A	C	L	A	I		E
M	C	A		U	M	E		I	E	N	N	S	N	A	M	A	T	V
A	H	M	Q	F	S	O	L		R	U	E	S	A	E	I	T	E	I
T	A	S	E	S	H	I	R		E	T	D	I	U	R	R	I	R	T
I	S	I		L	E			O	T	O	T	V	N	R	G	V	S	A
C	M	D	Q	U	E	R	I	E	S	R	U	E	F	U	L	E	E	R
H				U	N	E	L	E	U	E	S	X	N	S	I	Y	M	C
A			E		D	B	G	N	A	I	I	P	C	E	P		P	U
G		U		E	A	I	I	S	M	N	S	L	O	M	T		A	L
R	Q		L	F	L	A	U	E		E	O	O	Y	E	N	S	T	U
I		B	F	B	T	O	D	I	T	G	N	I	O	T	E	A	H	N
N	M	A	O	R	U	Y	A	R	R	A	G	T	B	I	N	F	Y	W
A			E	D		E	E	E		T	O	A	L	C	I	F	T	I
		C	R	V	V	V		V		E	R	T	I	U	M	L	I	T
	S	A	D	L	I			E			P	I	V	L	M	U	N	T
A		I	O	D		G		R				O	I	O	I	E	U	I
	R	S	E	C	A	M	I	R	G			N	O	U		N	P	N
A	B				Q	U	E	L	L	E	D		N	S		T	M	G
A	L	L	E	V	I	A	T	E	D	W	E	R	H	S			I	

ABSOLVE	CHASM	LUCRATIVE	QUERIES
AFFABLE	COY	MELEE	QUEUE
AFFLUENT	DEMISE	METICULOUS	REVERIES
ALLEVIATED	DISMAY	MILIEU	ROTUND
AMBLED	DIVERT	MOROSE	RUEFUL
APPREHENSIVELY	EMPATHY	NEGATE	SHEEN
APTNESS	EXPLOITATION	NUANCES	SHREWD
ARDUOUS	FEIGNED	OBLIGES	SQUALID
ARID	FURTIVE	OBLIVION	SURLY
ARRAY	GRIMACE	PALLIATIVE	SURREAL
ASCERTAIN	IMMINENT	PILGRIMAGE	TENETS
ATONE	IMPASSIVE	PRAGMATIC	TERSE
AUSTERE	IMPUNITY	PROGNOSIS	UNWITTING
CHAGRIN	LEER	QUELLED	VIGIL

VOCABULARY MATCHING 1 *The Kite Runner*

____ 1.	ABSOLVE	A.	Melancholy; gloomy
____ 2.	GRIMACE	B.	To call or bring into existence by or as if by magic
____ 3.	GUILELESS	C.	Agitation; perturbation; alarm
____ 4.	METICULOUS	D.	A file or line, especially of people waiting in turn
____ 5.	MOROSE	E.	Grave; strict; solemn; serious
____ 6.	NOVELTY	F.	Extremely steep
____ 7.	PERIPHERY	G.	Showing unease or fearfulness about something that might happen
____ 8.	PRECIPITOUS	H.	Discouraging through fear
____ 9.	QUEUE	I.	Sincere; honest; straightforward
____ 10.	FURTIVE	J.	Secret; sly; shifty
____ 11.	EXASPERATED	K.	Made easier to endure; lessened
____ 12.	ALLEVIATED	L.	Freed from guilt or blame
____ 13.	APPREHENSIVELY	M.	A facial expression that indicates disapproval or pain
____ 14.	ARRAY	N.	Extremely careful and precise; paying great attention to details
____ 15.	AUSTERE	O.	Made very angry or impatient; annoyed greatly
____ 16.	BLUDGEONED	P.	An impressively large number
____ 17.	CONJURE	Q.	Hit or overcame
____ 18.	DAUNTING	R.	Giving up; surrendering
____ 19.	DISMAY	S.	Something unique or new
____ 20.	RELINQUISHMENT	T.	The edge or outskirts

VOCABULARY MATCHING 1 ANSWER KEY *The Kite Runner*

L	1. ABSOLVE	A. Melancholy; gloomy
M	2. GRIMACE	B. To call or bring into existence by or as if by magic
I	3. GUILELESS	C. Agitation; perturbation; alarm
N	4. METICULOUS	D. A file or line, especially of people waiting in turn
A	5. MOROSE	E. Grave; strict; solemn; serious
S	6. NOVELTY	F. Extremely steep
T	7. PERIPHERY	G. Showing unease or fearfulness about something that might happen
F	8. PRECIPITOUS	H. Discouraging through fear
D	9. QUEUE	I. Sincere; honest; straightforward
J	10. FURTIVE	J. Secret; sly; shifty
O	11. EXASPERATED	K. Made easier to endure; lessened
K	12. ALLEVIATED	L. Freed from guilt or blame
G	13. APPREHENSIVELY	M. A facial expression that indicates disapproval or pain
P	14. ARRAY	N. Extremely careful and precise; paying great attention to details
E	15. AUSTERE	O. Made very angry or impatient; annoyed greatly
Q	16. BLUDGEONED	P. An impressively large number
B	17. CONJURE	Q. Hit or overcame
H	18. DAUNTING	R. Giving up; surrendering
C	19. DISMAY	S. Something unique or new
R	20. RELINQUISHMENT	T. The edge or outskirts

VOCABULARY MATCHING 2 *The Kite Runner*

____	1.	VALIANT	A.	Abounding or swarming with something, as with people
____	2.	GARRULOUS	B.	An environment or a setting; surroundings
____	3.	FUTILITY	C.	Foul and repulsive, as from lack of care or cleanliness; neglected and filthy
____	4.	EXPLOITATION	D.	To make up for; make amends for
____	5.	EPIPHANY	E.	Exemption from punishment, penalty, or harm
____	6.	CONTEMPTUOUS	F.	Round in shape; plump; fat
____	7.	CHAGRIN	G.	Showing or expressing contempt or disdain; scornful
____	8.	AUSTERE	H.	Boldly courageous; brave
____	9.	ANONYMITY	I.	A feeling of vexation, marked by disappointment or humiliation
____	10.	IMPUNITY	J.	Caution with regard to practical matters; regard for one's own interests
____	11.	MILIEU	K.	Freed from guilt or blame
____	12.	UNSCRUPULOUS	L.	Having no conscience or principles; oblivious to what is right or honorable
____	13.	TEEMING	M.	Extremely steep
____	14.	SQUALID	N.	The act of employing to the greatest possible advantage
____	15.	ROTUND	O.	Grave; strict; solemn; serious
____	16.	REDEMPTION	P.	Known widely and usually unfavorably known
____	17.	PRUDENCE	Q.	A sudden perception of or insight into the reality or essential meaning of something, usually initiated by some simple or commonplace occurrence or experience
____	18.	PRECIPITOUS	R.	Excessively talkative in a rambling, roundabout manner, especially about trivial matters
____	19.	NOTORIOUSLY	S.	Characterized by having no useful result; uselessness
____	20.	ABSOLVE	T.	The quality or state of being unknown or unacknowledged

VOCABULARY MATCHING 2 ANSWER KEY *The Kite Runner*

H	1. VALIANT	A. Abounding or swarming with something, as with people
R	2. GARRULOUS	B. An environment or a setting; surroundings
S	3. FUTILITY	C. Foul and repulsive, as from lack of care or cleanliness; neglected and filthy
N	4. EXPLOITATION	D. To make up for; make amends for
Q	5. EPIPHANY	E. Exemption from punishment, penalty, or harm
G	6. CONTEMPTUOUS	F. Round in shape; plump; fat
I	7. CHAGRIN	G. Showing or expressing contempt or disdain; scornful
O	8. AUSTERE	H. Boldly courageous; brave
T	9. ANONYMITY	I. A feeling of vexation, marked by disappointment or humiliation
E	10. IMPUNITY	J. Caution with regard to practical matters; regard for one's own interests
B	11. MILIEU	K. Freed from guilt or blame
L	12. UNSCRUPULOUS	L. Having no conscience or principles; oblivious to what is right or honorable
A	13. TEEMING	M. Extremely steep
C	14. SQUALID	N. The act of employing to the greatest possible advantage
F	15. ROTUND	O. Grave; strict; solemn; serious
D	16. REDEMPTION	P. Known widely and usually unfavorably known
J	17. PRUDENCE	Q. A sudden perception of or insight into the reality or essential meaning of something, usually initiated by some simple or commonplace occurrence or experience
M	18. PRECIPITOUS	R. Excessively talkative in a rambling, roundabout manner, especially about trivial matters
P	19. NOTORIOUSLY	S. Characterized by having no useful result; uselessness
K	20. ABSOLVE	T. The quality or state of being unknown or unacknowledged

VOCABULARY JUGGLE LETTERS 1 *The Kite Runner*

_______________ = 1. BAAFFEL
Pleasantly easy to approach and to talk to; friendly; cordial; warmly polite

_______________ = 2. TCOLNLNAANHY
Coolly unconcerned, indifferent; casually

_______________ = 3. OOLNIBVI
The state of being completely forgotten or unknown

_______________ = 4. VPEITALIAL
Relieving or soothing the symptoms of a disease or disorder without affecting a cure

_______________ = 5. RMITAPGAC
Dealing or concerned with facts or actual occurrences; practical

_______________ = 6. ECRNEETIC
State of being reluctant or reserved

_______________ = 7. UREASLR
Having the disorienting, hallucinatory quality of a dream; seeming unreal; fantastic

_______________ = 8. EERST
Brief and to the point

_______________ = 9. NTWTNIGIU
Unintentional; accidental; not knowing; unaware

_______________ = 10. TGANEE
To make ineffective or invalid; nullify

_______________ = 11. GNNIIADIOTN
Anger aroused by something unjust, mean, or unworthy

_______________ = 12. LATUFEFN
Generously supplied with money, property, or possessions; prosperous or rich

_______________ = 13. DARTOHPIE
Wasted; withered; shriveled

_______________ = 14. ONCRJEU
To call or bring into existence by or as if by magic

_______________ = 15. PMNUEOTUSOTC
Showing or expressing contempt or disdain; scornful

_______________ = 16. IVDRTE
To distract from serious occupation; entertain or amuse

_______________ = 17. PSTADAREXEE
Made very angry or impatient; annoyed greatly

_______________ = 18. LTIUTYFI
Characterized by having no useful result; uselessness

_______________ = 19. AAHDAHRLYZP
In a random manner; without care

_______________ = 20. VIILG
A watch kept during normal sleeping hours

VOCABULARY JUGGLE LETTERS 1 ANSWER KEY *The Kite Runner*

AFFABLE = 1. BAAFFEL
Pleasantly easy to approach and to talk to; friendly; cordial; warmly polite

NONCHALANTLY = 2. TCOLNLNAANHY
Coolly unconcerned, indifferent; casually

OBLIVION = 3. OOLNIBVI
The state of being completely forgotten or unknown

PALLIATIVE = 4. VPEITALIAL
Relieving or soothing the symptoms of a disease or disorder without affecting a cure

PRAGMATIC = 5. RMITAPGAC
Dealing or concerned with facts or actual occurrences; practical

RETICENCE = 6. ECRNEETIC
State of being reluctant or reserved

SURREAL = 7. UREASLR
Having the disorienting, hallucinatory quality of a dream; seeming unreal; fantastic

TERSE = 8. EERST
Brief and to the point

UNWITTING = 9. NTWTNIGIU
Unintentional; accidental; not knowing; unaware

NEGATE = 10. TGANEE
To make ineffective or invalid; nullify

INDIGNATION = 11. GNNIIADIOTN
Anger aroused by something unjust, mean, or unworthy

AFFLUENT = 12. LATUFEFN
Generously supplied with money, property, or possessions; prosperous or rich

ATROPHIED = 13. DARTOHPIE
Wasted; withered; shriveled

CONJURE = 14. ONCRJEU
To call or bring into existence by or as if by magic

CONTEMPTUOUS = 15. PMNUEOTUSOTC
Showing or expressing contempt or disdain; scornful

DIVERT = 16. IVDRTE
To distract from serious occupation; entertain or amuse

EXASPERATED = 17. PSTADAREXEE
Made very angry or impatient; annoyed greatly

FUTILITY = 18. LTIUTYFI
Characterized by having no useful result; uselessness

HAPHAZARDLY = 19. AAHDAHRLYZP
In a random manner; without care

VIGIL = 20. VIILG
A watch kept during normal sleeping hours

VOCABULARY JUGGLE LETTERS 2 *The Kite Runner*

_____________ = 1. LDBHNSAAUYE
Not concealed or disguised; obviously

_____________ = 2. MTNMINIE
Likely to occur at any moment; impending

_____________ = 3. SGULIEELS
Sincere; honest; straightforward

_____________ = 4. DEFCAA
An artificial or deceptive front

_____________ = 5. UECOJRN
To call or bring into existence by or as if by magic

_____________ = 6. UONBLDEEGD
Hit or overcame

_____________ = 7. VBEENEOLNEC
An inclination to perform kind, charitable acts

_____________ = 8. NEIYSEAPRPVELH
Showing unease or fearfulness about something that might happen

_____________ = 9. TAANVIBLME
Uncertain or unable to decide about what course to follow

_____________ = 10. NSNITONIUIA
An indirect or covert suggestion or hint especially of a derogatory nature

_____________ = 11. RCAVIUETL
Profitable; moneymaking

_____________ = 12. NITGMEE
Abounding or swarming with something, as with people

_____________ = 13. LUIDQAS
Foul and repulsive, as from lack of care or cleanliness; neglected and filthy

_____________ = 14. RSDHEW
Characterized by keen awareness, sharp intelligence, and often a sense of the practical

_____________ = 15. UODNTR
Round in shape; plump; fat

_____________ = 16. EQLLDUE
Pacified: quieted or suppressed

_____________ = 17. TIUOCRPSPIE
Extremely steep

_____________ = 18. GIAILRPMGE
A journey, especially a long one, made to some sacred place as an act of religious devotion

_____________ = 19. PEYPHRIRE
The edge or outskirts

_____________ = 20. EYDVASARR
Opponent; enemy

VOCABULARY JUGGLE LETTERS 2 ANSWER KEY *The Kite Runner*

UNABASHEDLY	= 1.	LDBHNSAAUYE Not concealed or disguised; obviously
IMMINENT	= 2.	MTNMINIE Likely to occur at any moment; impending
GUILELESS	= 3.	SGULIEELS Sincere; honest; straightforward
FACADE	= 4.	DEFCAA An artificial or deceptive front
CONJURE	= 5.	UECOJRN To call or bring into existence by or as if by magic
BLUDGEONED	= 6.	UONBLDEEGD Hit or overcame
BENEVOLENCE	= 7.	VBEENEOLNEC An inclination to perform kind, charitable acts
APPREHENSIVELY	= 8.	NEIYSEAPRPVELH Showing unease or fearfulness about something that might happen
AMBIVALENT	= 9.	TAANVIBLME Uncertain or unable to decide about what course to follow
INSINUATION	= 10.	NSNITONIUIA An indirect or covert suggestion or hint especially of a derogatory nature
LUCRATIVE	= 11.	RCAVIUETL Profitable; moneymaking
TEEMING	= 12.	NITGMEE Abounding or swarming with something, as with people
SQUALID	= 13.	LUIDQAS Foul and repulsive, as from lack of care or cleanliness; neglected and filthy
SHREWD	= 14.	RSDHEW Characterized by keen awareness, sharp intelligence, and often a sense of the practical
ROTUND	= 15.	UODNTR Round in shape; plump; fat
QUELLED	= 16.	EQLLDUE Pacified: quieted or suppressed
PRECIPITOUS	= 17.	TIUOCRPSPIE Extremely steep
PILGRIMAGE	= 18.	GIAILRPMGE A journey, especially a long one, made to some sacred place as an act of religious devotion
PERIPHERY	= 19.	PEYPHRIRE The edge or outskirts
ADVERSARY	= 20.	EYDVASARR Opponent; enemy

www.ingramcontent.com/pod-product-compliance
Lightning Source LLC
Chambersburg PA
CBHW082101090726
47910CB00008B/2551

9781602494862